fair isle &
nordic knits

fair isle &
nordic knits

nicki trench

25 projects inspired by
traditional colorwork designs

CICO BOOKS
LONDON NEW YORK

Published in 2014 by CICO Books
An imprint of Ryland Peters & Small Ltd
20–21 Jockey's Fields
London WC1R 4BW
519 Broadway, 5th Floor
New York, NY 10012

www.rylandpeters.com

10 9 8 7 6 5 4 3 2 1

A CIP catalog record for this book
is available from the Library of Congress
and the British Library.

ISBN: 978 1 78249 088 3

Printed in China

Editor: Marie Clayton
Designer: Alison Fenton
Photographers: Holly Joliffe, Emma Mitchell
Stylists: Nel Haynes, Harriet de Winton

For digital editions, visit
www.cicobooks.com/apps.php

contents

Introduction 6

introduction

My Fair Isle experience started pretty early; my grandmother was a prolific Fair Isle knitter and one of my earliest knitting memories is being shown how to make little sample squares of Fair Isle. I loved it and it has always fulfilled my need to work with color—out of all the knitting I've practiced, Fair Isle is my favorite and the finished effect is always really satisfying, no matter how imperfect it has been.

Needless to say, Fair Isle is a slow process, particularly if you are just starting out. It doesn't grow very fast, but each row or round feels like an enormous achievement. It's not the type of knitting you can do if you're watching a complex crime drama on television—save it for when you are watching your favorite soaps, or listening to music or the radio. Untangling the different strands of colored yarn is all part of the process, so don't regard this as a chore—I've come to really enjoy it, because it breaks up the times when you need to be concentrating so hard on the charts.

Fair Isle is not just for the experienced knitter. Although there are a few special techniques that are useful (see our techniques section on page 106), my philosophy has always been to jump in and give it a go. Like any craft, it really doesn't have to be perfect —and if a stitch goes out of line here and there, weigh up whether you really need to undo it before you dive in and start pulling your work out. One thing to note is that the patterns give both imperial and metric measurements, but they are not exact conversions so it is important to stick to one set only.

Fair Isle is a knitting technique in which stitches in a row are worked in different colors to create patterns that are often quite complex. Traditional Fair Isle uses only two colors across one row, but modern designs can use more colors, often with long "stretches" between. A mix of stranding and weaving techniques (see pages 119–120) is used to control the yarns not in use.

Traditional Fair Isle is worked on circular needles in the round using stockinette (stocking) stitch, to create a tube. This means you only need to knit and not purl and work only on the right side. At openings such as armholes, a bridge of stitches known as a steek is worked so that the tube continues without interruption. After completing the tube the knitted fabric was cut through the steeks, so that stitches could be picked up around the opening to create additional pieces such as the arms. However, you can create beautiful garments and home projects by knitting in flat rows and using the usual seams to join pieces and in this book I have included Fair Isle and Nordic designs, created using both circular and straight row knitting.

The fashion for Nordic and vintage style has really increased the popularity of Fair Isle and color knitting and in this book you will find projects for all levels. If you're a beginner, try some of the easy projects such as the Swiss Check Scarf on page 62 or the Cafetière Cover on page 92. If you want to move on to the next level, there are some lovely projects in the For the Home section like the Nordic Blue Pillow Cover, Bunting, or Knitted Sampler; or, if you've mastered the basic techniques and would like to try something more challenging, try knitting the garments or try Fair Isle in a mohair yarn by tackling the Light as a Feather Scarf on page 60. My advice, though, would be to choose the projects you love and give them a go. It may be a slow journey, but it will be a very enjoyable one.

Traditionally Fair Isle is knitted using a firmly twisted yarn, which gives a more consistent gauge (tension) than soft or loosely spun yarns. However, I'm a big fan of soft yarns—they are simply more comfortable and my belief is that the revival of knitting and crochet in recent years is due to the soft yarns that are on the market. In this book I've used mainly Debbie Bliss Yarns, which are soft and come in more contemporary colors.

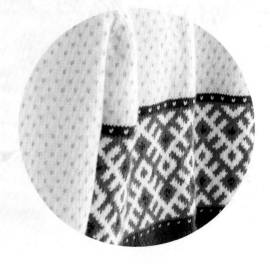

CHAPTER 1
to wear

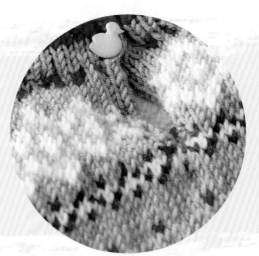

pretty in pink cardigan

Who can resist this little cardigan—if you don't fancy the pink, try out some different color combinations. A baby cardigan is a fairly speedy project and this makes a fantastic gift for a new baby.

materials

- Debbie Bliss Baby Cashmerino (55% merino wool/33% microfiber/12% cashmere) light worsted (DK) yarn
    3 x 1¾ oz (50 g) balls – approx.137 yd (125 m) per ball – of shade 006 Candy Pink (pink) (MC)
    ⅛ x 1¾ oz (50 g) ball – approx. 17.5 yd (16 m) – each of shades 202   Light Blue, 059 Mallard (blue-green), 101 Ecru (off-white)
- US size 2 (2.75 mm) and US size 3 (3.25 mm) straight knitting needles
- US size 2 (2.75 mm), US size 2/3 (3 mm) and US size 3 (3.25 mm) circular knitting needles
- 2 stitch holders
- Yarn sewing needle
- 6 small buttons

gauge (tension)

25 sts and 34 rows over 4 in. (10 cm) square working st st using US size 3 (3.25 mm) needles.

finished size

To fit ages: 3–6:**6–9**:9–12 months
Chest measurement: 19¾:**22**:24½ in. (50:**56**:62 cm)
Length to shoulder: 8¾:**9½**:10¼ in. (22:**24**:26 cm)
Sleeve length: 5½:**6¼**:7 in. (14:**16**:18 cm)

Notes

Chart is read right to left on odd-numbered (RS) rows and left to right on even-numbered (WS) rows.
Strand colors not in use loosely on WS of work.

Back and Fronts

(make 1)
Using US size 2 (2.75 mm) straight needles and MC, cast on 125:**141**:157 sts.
Rib row 1: P1, *k1, p1; rep from * to end.
Rib row 2: K1, *p1, k1; rep from * to end.
Rep the last 2 rows 2:**2**:3 times more.
Change to US size 3 (3.25 mm) needles.
Beg with a k row, work in st st until work measures 4¾:**5**:5½ in. (12:**13**:14 cm) from cast-on edge, ending with a WS row.
Divide for Back and Fronts:
Next row: K31:**35**:39, leave these sts on a holder for Right Front, k next 63:**71**:79 sts and leave these sts on a holder for Back, k to end.
Left front:
Work straight on last set of 31:**35**:39 sts for 2:**4**:6 rows, so ending with a k row.
Yoke shaping:
Bind (cast) off 6 sts at beg (front edge) of next row, 3 sts at beg of 3 foll alt rows, then 2 sts on 3:**4**:5 foll alt rows.
Now dec 1 st at beg of every foll alt row until 3:**5**:7 sts rem.
Cont straight until Left Front measures 8¾:**9½**:10¼ in. (22:**24**: 26 cm) from cast-on edge, ending at armhole edge.
Shape shoulder:
Bind (cast) off.

Back

With WS facing, rejoin yarn to next st on back holder, p63:**71**:79.
Work straight on these sts for 2:**4**:6 rows.
Yoke shaping:
Next row: K25:**29**:33, turn and work on these sts.
Bind (cast) off 3 sts at beg of next row, and 2 foll alt rows, then 2 sts on 3:**4**:5 foll alt rows.
Now dec 1 st at beg of every foll alt row until 3:**5**:7 sts rem.
Cont straight until back measures 8¾:**9½**:10¼ in. (22:**24**:26 cm) from cast-on edge, ending at armhole edge.

Shape shoulder:
Bind (cast) off.
With RS facing, slip center 13 sts onto a holder, rejoin yarn to rem 25:**29**:33 sts, k to end.
Next row: P.
Complete to match first side of Back.

Right Front

With WS facing, rejoin yarn to next st on Right Front, p to end.
Work straight on these 31:**35**:39 sts for 2:**4**:6 rows.
Yoke shaping:
Bind (cast) off 6 sts at beg of next row, 3 sts at beg of 3 foll alt rows, then 2 sts on 3:**4**:5 foll alt rows.
Now dec 1 st at beg of every foll alt row until 3:**5**:7 sts rem.
Cont straight until front measures 8¾:**9½**:10¼ in. (22:**24**:26 cm) from cast-on edge, ending at armhole edge.
Shape shoulder:
Bind (cast) off.

Yoke

Join shoulder seams using mattress stitch. With RS facing and using US size 3 (3.25 mm) circular needle and MC, pick up and knit 40:**44**:48 sts on Right Front neck edge, 35:**39**:43 sts on right Back neck edge, k across 13 sts from stitch holder, pick up 35:**39**:43 on left Back neck edge and 40:**44**:48 sts on Left Front neck edge. (163:**179**:195 sts)
Beg with a p row, work 3 rows st st.
Dec row: K5, k2tog, *k6, k2tog; rep from * to last 4 sts, k4. (143:**157**:171 sts)
Next row: P.
Work Rows 1–2 from Chart 1, starting at st 1 and ending at st 5.
Dec row: Using MC, k4, k2tog, *k5, k2tog; rep from * to last 4 sts, k4. (123:**135**:147 sts)
Work rows 1–5 of Chart 2. NB: This Chart starts on a p row, so work row from left to right.
Change to US size 2/3 (3 mm) circular needle.
Work Rows 6–9 from Chart 2.
Dec row (Row 10 of Chart): K3, *k2tog, k5, k2tog, k3; rep from * to end. (103:**113**:123 sts)
Work rows 1–2 from Chart 1, starting at st 2 and ending at st 4.
Cont in MC only.
Next row: P.
Dec row: K3 *k2tog, k3; rep from * to end. (83:**91**:99 sts)
Next row: P.
Dec row: K3, *k2tog, k2; rep from * to end. (63:**69**:75 sts)
Next row: P.
Change to US size 2 (2.75 mm) circular needle.
Rib row 1: K1, *p1, k1; rep from * to end.
Rib row 2: P1, *k1, p1; rep from * to end.
Rep last two rows once more.
Bind (cast) off.

Button Band

With RS facing and using US size 2 (2.75 mm) straight needles and MC, pick up and knit 55:**61**:67 sts along Left Front edge.
Work 4 rows rib as given for Back and Fronts.
Bind (cast) off in rib.

Buttonhole Band

With RS facing and using US size 2 (2.75 mm) straight needles and MC, pick up and knit 55:**61**:67 sts along Right Front edge.
Work 1 row rib as given for Back and Fronts.
Buttonhole row: Rib 2, [rib 2tog, yf, rib 8:**9**:10 sts] 5 times, rib 2tog, yf, rib 1:**2**:3 sts. Rib 2 rows.
Bind (cast) off in rib.

Sleeves

(make 2)

Using US size 2 (2.75 mm) straight needles and MC, cast on 36:**40**:44 sts.

Work 6:**8**:10 rows in [k1, p1] rib.

Change to US size 3 (3.25 mm) needles.

Beg with a k row work in st st, inc 1 st at each end of 3rd and every foll 4th row until there are 52:**58**:62 sts.

Cont straight until sleeve measures 5½:**6¼**:7 in. (14:**16**:18 cm) from cast-on edge, ending with a p row.

Bind (cast) off.

Finishing

Join sleeve seams using mattress stitch. Sew sleeves into armholes using mattress stitch.

Sew on buttons to match buttonhole positions.

Chart 1

2 stitch
repeat

Chart 2

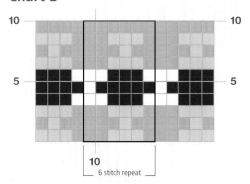

6 stitch repeat

Key to colors

■ Candy Pink (pink)

■ Light Blue

■ Mallard (blue-green)

□ Ecru (off-white)

nordic blue sweater

Using contemporary colors makes all the difference on this gorgeous yoked sweater. It's made using a worsted (Aran) weight in a mix of cashmere and merino wool to create a really warm and luxurious garment.

materials

- Debbie Bliss Cashmerino Aran (55% merino wool/33% microfiber/ 12% cashmere) worsted (Aran) yarn
  7:**8**:9:**10**:11 x 1¾ oz (50 g) balls – approx. 98.5 yd (90 m) per ball – of shade 056 Mallard (blue-green) (MC)
  1:**1**:1:**1**:1 x 1¾ oz (50 g) ball – approx. 98.5 yd (90 m) – each of shades 048 Burnt Orange (A), 047 Aqua (turquoise) (B), 502 Lime (green) (C), 053 Rose (pale pink) (D), 202 Silver (E)
  1:**1**:2:**2**:2 x 1¾ oz (50 g) balls – approx. 98.5 yd (90 m) per ball – of shade 101 Ecru (off-white) (F)
- US size 4 (3.5 mm) and US size 7 (4.5 mm) circular needles
- US size 4 (3.5 mm) and US size 7 (4.5 mm) double-pointed needles
- Yarn sewing needle

gauge (tension)

18 sts and 24 rows to 10cm square working st st using US size 7 (4.5 mm) needles.

finished size

To fit size: 32:**34**:36:**38**:40 in. (81:**86**:91:**97**:102 cm)
Bust measurement: 33½:**35**:38¾:**42¼**:45¾ in. (85:**89**:98:**107**:116 cm)
Length to shoulder: 22:**22¾**:23¼:**24**:24¾ in. (55:**56**:58:**60**:62 cm)

Notes

Chart 1 is read right to left on odd-numbered (RS) rows and left to right on even-numbered (WS) rows.
Charts 2, 3, and 4 are read right to left on every row.
Strand colors not in use loosely on WS of work.

Body

Using US size 4 (3.5 mm) circular needle and MC, cast on 152:**160**:176:**192**:208 sts. Join in a circle and work *k1, p1* rib for 1½ in. (4 cm).
Change to US size 7 (4.5 mm) circular needle and work patt from Chart 1 in st st.
When patt is complete, cont with MC until body measures 14¾:**15**: 15¾:**16¾**:17½ in. (37:**38**:40:**42**:44 cm) from cast-on edge.

Next row: Bind (cast) off 4:**5**:6:**7**:8 sts, k68:**70**:76:**82**:88 sts including st on RH needle after bind (cast) off, bind (cast) off 8:**10**:12:**14**:16 sts, k to last 4:**5**:6:**7**:8 sts, bind (cast) off.
Fasten off. (136:**140**:152:**164**:176 sts)
Set aside and work sleeves.

Sleeves

Using US size 4 (3.5 mm) dpns and MC, cast on 38:**40**:42:**44**:46 sts. Join in a circle and work *k1, p1* rib for 1½ in. (4 cm), inc 0:**0**:0:**0**:2 sts in last round. (38:**40**:42:**44**:48 sts)
Change to US size 7 (4.5 mm) dpns and work patt from Chart 1 in st st (patt repeat is not complete in all sizes).
When patt is finished, cont with MC.
Inc 1 st after first st and 1 st before last st of round on next and every 10th:**9th**:8th:**7th**:7th round to 56:**60**:64:**68**:72 sts.
Work straight until sleeve measures 16¾:**17**:17¼:**17½**:17¾ in. (42.5:**43**:43.5:**44**:44.5 cm).
Bind (cast) off 4:**5**:6:**7**:8 sts, k to last 4:**5**:6:**7**:8 sts, bind (cast) off. (48:**50**:52:**54**:56 sts)
Work second sleeve.

Yoke

Join body and sleeves:
Using US size 7 (4.5 mm) circular needle and MC, k sts from first sleeve, then from front, second sleeve and back.
(232:**240**:256:**272**:288 sts)
Work 5 rounds.

Chart 1

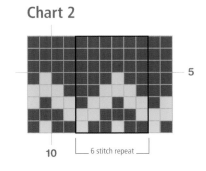

5 | | 5

20 | 10

8 stitch repeat

Chart 2

5

10 | 6 stitch repeat

Chart 3

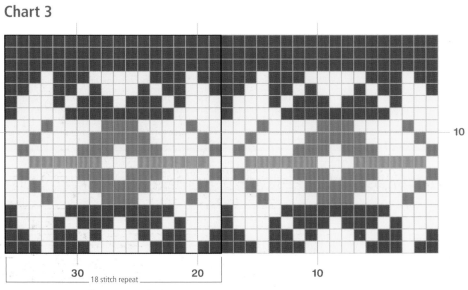

10

30 | 20 | 10

18 stitch repeat

Chart 4

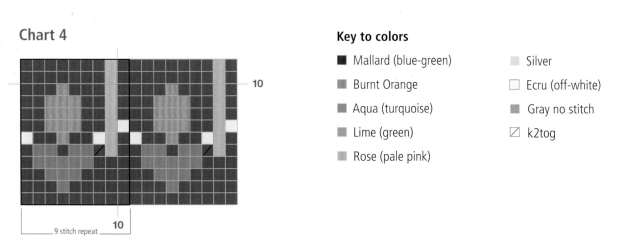

10

9 stitch repeat | 10

Key to colors

- ■ Mallard (blue-green)
- ■ Burnt Orange
- ■ Aqua (turquoise)
- ■ Lime (green)
- ■ Rose (pale pink)

- ■ Silver
- ☐ Ecru (off-white)
- ■ Gray no stitch
- ☑ k2tog

Round 6: [K2:**0**:5:**4**:0, *k6:**6**:5:**6**:6, k2tog, rep from * 7:**7**:9:**8**:9 times, k2:**0**:4:**4**:0, *k6:**6**:5:**6**:6, k2tog, rep from * 7:**8**:8:**8**:9 times] twice. 204:**210**:222:**240**:252 sts

Start to work from Chart 2 (dec as indicated below).

Round 8 of chart: [k7:**5**:8:**8**:5, k2tog] 3:**30**:2:**24**:36 times, [k6:**0**:7:**0**:0, k2tog] 6:**0**:9:**0**:0 times, [k7:**0**:8:**0**:0, k2tog] 6:**0**:3:**0**:0 times, [k6:**0**:7:**0**:0, k2tog] 6:**0**:9:**0**:0 times, [k7:**0**:3:**0**:0, k2tog] 3:**0**:1:**0**:0 times. (180:**180**:198:**216**:216 sts)

Work Chart 3.

Round 17 of chart: [k3:**3**:3:**4**:4, k2tog] 36:**36**:7:**36**:36 times, [k0:**0**:6:**0**:0, k2tog] 0:**0**:3:**0**:0 times, [k0:**0**:3:**0**:0, k2tog] 0:**0**:15:**0**:0 times, [k0:**0**:6:**0**:0, k2tog] 0:**0**:3:**0**:0 times, [k0:**0**:8:**0**:0, k2tog] 0:**0**:8:**0**:0 times. (144:**144**:162:**180**:180 sts)

Work Chart 4.

Note charted decreases in Round 5. (128:**128**:144:**160**:160 sts)

Round 12 of chart: *K2tog, k2; rep from * to end. (96:**96**:108:**120**:120 sts)

Neckband:

Change to US size 4 (3.5 mm) circular needles and using MC work one round.

Next round 1st and 2nd sizes: K5:**7**:–:–:–, k2tog, *K10:**14**:–:–:–, k2tog, rep from * 7:**5**:–:–:– times, k5:**7**:–:–:–. (88:**90**:–:–:– sts)

Next round 3rd, 4th and 5th sizes: *K4, k2tog; rep from * to end. (–:–:90:**100**:100 sts)

Work *k1, p1* rib for 3¼ in. (8 cm).

Bind (cast) off loosely.

Finishing

Sew underarm bound- (cast-) off edges tog and sew in loose ends. Fold neckband in half to inside and slipstitch in place.

two-tone sweater

This style based on two colors, with the color change at the bust, was very popular in the early 1900s. I have tried to keep the pattern simple, so it's an ideal project for those just starting out on Fair Isle. If you change the color combinations, I've found that one bright and one pale works best.

materials

- Debbie Bliss Rialto DK (100% extra-fine merino wool) light worsted (DK) yarn
  6:**7**:8:**8**:9:**11**:11:**12** x 1¾ oz (50 g) balls – approx. 115 yd (105 m) per ball – of shade 56 Tangerine (orange) (A)
  4:**5**:5:**6**:6:**7**:8:**8** x 1¾ oz (50 g) balls – approx. 115 yd (105 m) per ball – of shade 019 Duck Egg (pale blue) (B)
- US size 4 (3.5 mm) and US 5 (3.75 mm) straight knitting needles
- US size 4 (3.5 mm) circular needle
- 3 stitch holders
- Yarn sewing needle

gauge (tension)

23 sts x 32 rows over 4 in. (10 cm) square working st st using US size 5 (3.75 mm) needles.

finished size

Women's sizes: 1:**2**:3:**4**:5
To fit bust: 34:**36**:38:**40**:42 in. (85:**90**:95:**100**:105 cm)
Bust measurement: 36:**38**:40:**42**:44 in. (91:**96**:101.5:**107**:112 cm)
Length to shoulder: 20½:**21¼**:22:**23¼**:23¾ in. (52:**54**:56:**59**:60 cm)
Sleeve length: 15:**15¼**:15¼:**16**:16½ in. (38:**39**:39:**40.5**:42 cm)

Men's sizes: **6**:7:**8**
To fit chest: **44**:46:**48** in. (**110**:115:**120** cm)
Chest measurement: **46¾**:49:**51¼** in. (**117**:122.5:**128** cm)
Length to shoulder: **27½**:28:**28½** in. (**70**:71:**72** cm)
Sleeve length: **19¾**:20:**20¾** in. (**50**:51:**52.5** cm)

Notes

Chart is read right to left on odd-numbered (RS) rows and left to right on even-numbered (WS) rows.
Strand colors not in use loosely on WS of work.

Back

Using A and US size 4 (3.5 mm) straight needles, cast on 105:**111**:117:**123**:129:**135**:141:**147** sts.
Row 1: (RS): *K1, p1; rep from * to last st, k1.
Row 2: *P1, k1; rep from * to last st, p1.
These two rows form single rib (k1, p1) patt.
Cont to work in single rib as set until work measures 2:**2**:2:**2**:2:**2¾**:2¾:**2¾** in. (5:**5**:5:**5**:5:**7**:7:**7** cm) from cast-on edge, ending with a WS row.
Change to US size 5 (3.75 mm) needles.
Next row (RS): K to end of row.
Next row: P to end of row.
The last two rows form st st patt.
Cont to work in st st until work measures 11½:**11½**:11¾:**12½**:12½:**15**:15¼:**15¼** in. (29:**29**:30:**32**:32:**38**:39:**39** cm) from cast-on edge, ending with a WS row.
Beg with a k row, work 14 rows in st st following Chart starting and ending where indicated, introducing yarn B as shown on Chart.
Shape armholes:
Cont in B.
Bind (cast) off 4:**4**:6:**6**:6:**7**:7:**7** sts at beg of next two rows.
Bind (cast) off 2 sts at beg of next 8:**8**:6:**6**:6:**9**:9:**9** rows.
Dec 1 st at each end of next –:**1**:3:**5**:7:**5**:6:**8** alt rows.
(81:**85**:87:**89**:91:**93**:97:**99** sts)**
All sizes:
Cont to work in st st until Back measures 19½:**20½**:21¼:**22½**:22¾:**26¾**:27¼:**28** in. (50:**52**:54:**57**:58:**68**:69:**71** cm) from cast-on edge, ending with a WS row.
Shape shoulders for each size as indicated:
Bind (cast) off 7 sts at beg of next 6:**4**:2:–:–:–:–:– rows.
Bind (cast) off 8 sts at beg of next –:**2**:4:**6**:4:**4**:–:– rows.
Bind (cast) off 9 sts at beg of next –:–:–:–:2:**2**:6:**6** rows.
Slip rem 39:**41**:41:**41**:41:**43**:43:**45** sts onto a st holder.

Front

Work as given for Back until **.

Cont to work in st st until Front measures 17¼:**17½**:18:**18¾**:19: **22½**:22½:**23** in. (43.5:**44**:45.5:**47.5**:48:**57**:57:**58** cm) from cast-on edge, ending with a WS row.

Shape front neck:

Next row (RS): K28:**29**:30:**31**:33:**34**:35:**36**, turn, leave rem unworked sts on st holder.

Cont to work in st st on these 28:**29**:30:**31**:33:**34**:35:**36** sts only (left front of neck), at the same time dec 1 st at neck edge of next 7:**7**:7:**7**:8:**9**:8:**9** alt rows. (21:**22**:23:**24**:25:**25**:27:**27** sts)

Cont to work in st st without shaping until Front matches Back to start of shoulder shaping, ending with a WS row.

Shape shoulders for each size as indicated:

Bind (cast) off 7 sts at beg of next 3:**2**:1:–:–:–:–:– alt rows.
Bind (cast) off 8 sts at beg of next –:**1**:2:**3**:2:**2**:–:– alt rows.
Bind (cast) off 9 sts at beg of next –:–:–:–:1:**1**:3:**3** alt rows.

All sizes:

Leave center 25:**27**:27:**27**:25:**25**:27:**27** sts on a st holder and rejoin yarn to unworked sts to work right front of neck.
Knit 1 row.
Work to match left front of neck, reversing all shaping.

Sleeves

(make 2)

Using A and US size 4 (3.5 mm) straight needles, cast on 51:**51**:53:**53**:55:**55**:57:**57** sts.

Work 2:**2**:2:**2**:2:**2¾**:2¾:**2¾** in. (5:**5**:5:**5**:5:**7**:7:**7** cm) in single rib, ending with a WS row.

Change to US size 5 (3.75 mm) straight needles.

Work 4:**4**:4:**4**:4:**6**:6:**6** rows in st st, starting with a k row.

Inc 1 st at each end of next and every foll sixth row 12:**10**:7:**6**:8:**14**:13:**13** times in all.

Inc 1 st at each end of every foll fourth row 5:**9**:13:**16**:14:**10**:11:**12** times in all. (85:**89**:93:**97**:99:**103**:105:**107** sts)

Work 1:**1**:3:**1**:1:**1**:1:**1** rows.

Beg with a k row, work 14 rows in st st foll Chart starting and ending where indicated, introducing B as shown on Chart.

Shape sleeve top:

Cont to work in st st using B only, bind (cast) off 4:**4**:6:**6**:6:**7**:7:**7** sts at beg of next 2 rows.

Bind (cast) off 4:**4**:2:**2**:2:**3**:3:**3** sts at beg of next 2 rows.

Row 1 (RS): K1, skpo, k to last 3 sts, k2tog, k1.
Row 2: P to end of row.

Rep last two rows until 31:**33**:35:**37**:37:**37**:37:**39** sts rem.

Bind (cast) off 3 sts at beg of next 4 rows.

Bind (cast) off rem 19:**21**:23:**25**:25:**25**:25:**27** sts.

Finishing

Sew in ends on wrong side of work.
Join shoulder seams.

Neckband:

Using US 4 (3.5 mm) circular needle and B, with RS facing and starting at left should seam, pick up 26:**28**:30:**32**:34:**36**:40:**42** sts down left front neck, 25:**27**:27:**27**:25:**25**:27:**27** from st holder at center front neck, 26:**28**:30:**32**:34:**36**:40:**42** sts up right front neck to right shoulder seam, 39:**41**:41:**41**:41:**43**:43:**45** sts from st holder at center back neck. (116:**124**:128:**132**:134:**140**:150:**156** sts)

Working in rounds, cont to work in single rib for 6:**6**:6:**6**:6:**10**:10:**10** rounds.

Bind (cast) off loosely in rib.

Making up:

Join side and sleeve seams, sew in sleeves.

Women's chart

Key to colors

- ■ Tangerine (orange)
- ▩ Duck Egg (pale blue)

40   30   20   16 stitch repeat   10

End back size 2
End back size 3 & sleeve size 1
End sleeve size 2
End back size 4
End sleeve size 3
End back size 5 & sleeve size 4
End sleeve size 5
End back size 1

Start back size 2
Start back size 3 & sleeve size 1
Start sleeve size 2
Start back size 4
Start sleeve size 3
Start back size 5 & sleeve size 4
Start sleeve size 5
Start back size 1

Men's chart

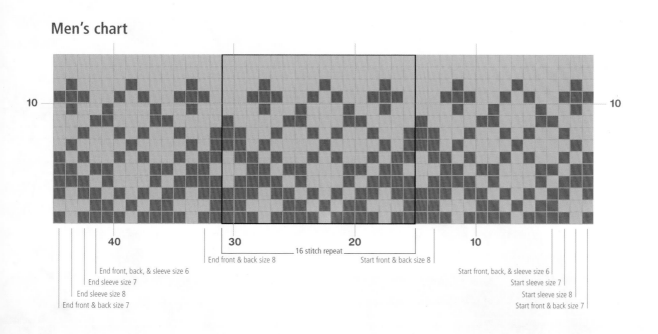

ducks in a row

This vest has the perfect shape and the most beautiful designs and is a must for any baby. The colors work equally well for a girl or boy, but feel free to choose your own shades.

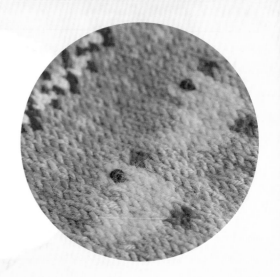

materials

- Debbie Bliss Baby Cashmerino (55% merino wool/33% microfiber/12% cashmere) light worsted (DK) yarn
    1:**2**:2:**2** x 1¾ oz (50 g) balls – approx. 137 yd (125 m) per ball – of shade 09 Slate (gray) (A)
    1:**1**:1:**1** x 1¾ oz (50 g) balls – approx. 137 yd (125 m) per ball – each of shades 034 Bright Red (B), 101 Ecru (off-white) (C), 083 Butter (yellow) (D), 059 Mallard (blue-green) (E), 067 Sienna (orange) (F), 068 Peach Melba (peach) (G), 081 Emerald (green) (H), 071 Pool (light blue) (J)
- US size 2/3 (3 mm) and US size 3 (3.25 mm) straight knitting needles
- US size 2/3 (3 mm) circular needle
- 2 small duck-shaped buttons
- Stitch holder and yarn sewing needle

gauge (tension)

25 sts x 34 rows over 4 in. (10 cm) square working Fair Isle patt in st st using US size 3 (3.25 mm) needles.

finished size

To fit ages: 3–6:**6–9**:9–12:**12–18** months
Chest measurement: 19:**20**:22:**24** in. (48:**51**:56:**61** cm)
Length to shoulder: 9½:**10¼**:11:**11¾** in. (24:**26**:28:**30** cm)

Notes

Chart is read right to left on odd-numbered (RS) rows and left to right on even-numbered (WS) rows.
Only oddments of yarns D to J are required.
For 3–6 months size finish on Fair Isle Chart row 68. For all other sizes cont in A when Chart is complete.

Back

Using B and US size 2/3 (3 mm) straight needles, cast on 62:**65**:71:**77** sts.
Row 1 (RS): K2, [p1, k2]; rep to end.
Row 2: P2, [k1, p2]; rep to end.
Change to A and cont in rib as set for a further 13 rows.
Dec row (WS): Dec 1:**0**:0:**0** st in center of row. (61:**65**:71:**77** sts)
Change to US size 3 (3.25 mm) needles.
Beg with a k row, work 0:**0**:2:**6** rows in st st.
Cont in st st, work Chart starting and finishing where indicated.
Cont working from Chart as set in st st until row 32:**36**:38:**40** is complete.
Shape armholes:
Bind (cast) off 4:**4**:5:**5** sts at beg of next 2 rows. (53:**57**:61:**67** sts)
Dec 1 st at each end of next row and 4:**4**:5:**5** foll right side rows. (43:**47**:49:**55** sts)**
Cont straight in st st until Chart row 50:**56**:60:**64** is complete.
Divide for back opening:
Next row: K20:**22**:23:**26**, turn and cast on 3 sts.
Cont on these 23:**25**:26:**29** sts only for first side of neck, leave rem sts on a spare needle.
Next row (WS): P2, k1, p to end.
Next row: K to last 3 sts, p1, k2.
Rep these 2 rows until Chart row 64:**70**:74:**78** is complete.
NB for the largest size, you will have worked 4 plain rows after end of Chart.
Shape back neck:
Next 2 rows: K to last 8:**9**:9:**10** sts, slip these sts onto a holder, turn and p to end.
Next 2 rows: K to last 5 sts, slip these sts onto same holder, turn and p to end.
Bind (cast) off rem 10:**11**:12:**14** sts for shoulder.
With RS facing, rejoin yarn to sts on spare needle, k2, p1, k to end.
Row 1 (WS): P to last 3 sts, k1, p2.
Row 2: K2, p1, k to end.
Rep the last 2 rows twice more, then Row 1 again.

Buttonhole row (RS): K2, yf, k2tog, k to end.
Rep rows 1 and 2 until Chart row 64:**70**:74:**78** is complete.
NB for the largest size, you will have worked 4 plain rows after end of Chart.
Shape back neck:
Next row (RS): K2, p1, k5:**6**:6:**7** and slip these 8:**9**:9:**10** sts onto a holder, k to end.
P1 row.
Next row: K5 and slip these sts onto the same holder, k to end.
P1 row.
Bind (cast) off rem 10:**11**:12:**14** sts for shoulder.

Front

Work as Back to **.
Cont straight in st st until Chart row 46:**52**:58:**60** is complete.
Shape neck:
Next row: K16:**17**:18:**20** sts, turn and cont on these sts only for first side, leave rem sts on a spare needle.
Next row (WS): P1, p2tog, p to end.
K1 row.
Rep the last 2 rows until 10:**11**:12:**14** sts rem.
Work straight until Front measures same as Back to shoulder, ending with a p row.
Bind (cast) off.
With RS facing, slip center 11:**13**:13:**15** sts onto a holder, rejoin yarn to rem sts, k to end.

Next row: P to last 3 sts, p2tog tbl, p1.
K1 row.
Rep the last 2 rows until 10:**11**:12:**14** sts rem.
Work straight until Front measures same as Back to shoulder, ending with a p row.
Bind (cast) off.

Neckband

Join shoulder seams.
With RS facing, using A and US size 2/3 (3 mm) circular needle, work across 13:**14**:14:**15** sts on left Back neck holder as follows: k2, p1, k10:**11**:11:**12**, then pick up 2 sts at Back neck edge to shoulder, and k18:**19**:19:**20** sts down left side of Front neck, work across 11:**13**:13:**15** sts on Front neck holder, pick up and k18:**19**:19:**20** sts up right side of Front neck, 2 sts from Back neck edge, then work across 13:**14**:14:**15** sts on right Back neck holder as follows: k10:**11**:11:**12**, p1, k2. (77:**83**:83:**89** sts)
Row 1 (WS): P2, [k1, p2] to end.
Buttonhole row: K2, yf, k2tog, k1, [p1 k2] to end.
Row 3: As Row 1.
Change to B.
Row 4: K2, [p1 k2] to end.
Row 5: As Row 1.
Bind (cast) off in rib.

Armbands

With RS facing, using A and US size 2/3 (3 mm) straight needles, pick up and k62:**68**:74:**80** sts evenly around armhole edge.
Row 1 (WS): P2, [k1, p2] to end.
Row 2: K2, [p1, k2] to end.
Row 3: As Row 1.
Change to B and rep Rows 2 and 3 once more.
Bind (cast) off in rib.

Finishing

Join side and armband seams. Stitch cast-on sts at back opening behind buttonhole band. Sew on buttons to match buttonhole positions.

Key to colors

- Slate (gray)
- Bright Red
- Ecru (off-white)
- Butter (yellow)
- Mallard (blue-green)
- Sienna (orange)
- Peach Melba (peach)
- Emerald (green)
- Pool (light blue)

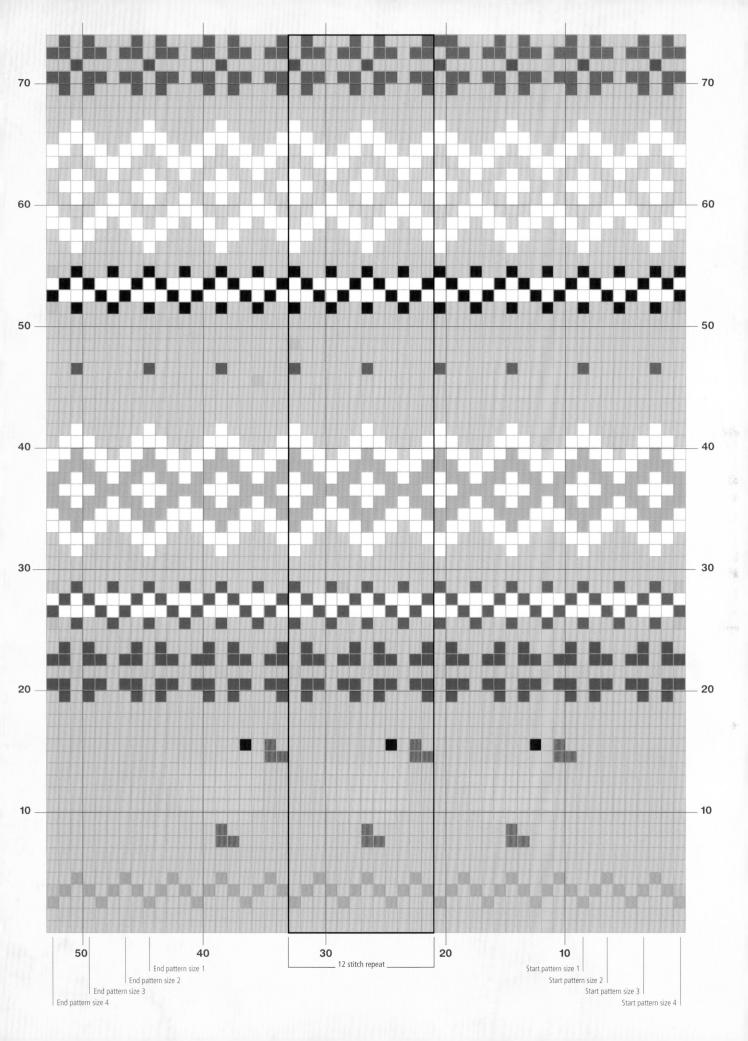

70

60

50

40

30

20

10

50

40

30

20

10

70

60

50

40

30

20

10

End pattern size 1
End pattern size 2
End pattern size 3
End pattern size 4

12 stitch repeat

Start pattern size 1
Start pattern size 2
Start pattern size 3
Start pattern size 4

rose garden cardigan

This charming and colorful cardigan has Fair Isle on the front, back, and sleeves, so it is a project that will take a little while to make, but it will be well worth the effort. If these colors don't appeal, choose your own shades.

materials

- Debbie Bliss Baby Cashmerino (55% merino wool/33% microfiber/12% cashmere) light worsted (DK) yarn
  6:**6**:7:**7** x 1¾ oz (50 g) balls – approx. 137 yd (125 m) per ball – of shade 070 Royal (blue) (MC)
  2 x 1¾ oz (50 g) balls – approx. 137 yd (125 m) per ball – each of shades 001 Primrose (yellow) (A), 081 Emerald (green) (B), 068 Peach Melba (peach) (C), 078 Lipstick (deep pink) (D), 101 Ecru (off-white) (E), 006 Candy Pink (pale pink) (F)
- US size 2/3 (3 mm) and US size 3 (3.25 mm) knitting needles
- Yarn sewing needle
- 9 pearl buttons

gauge (tension)

29 sts x 32 rows over 4 in. (10 cm) square working Fair Isle patt in st st using US size 3 (3.25 mm) needles.

finished size

To fit bust: 32–34:**36–38**:40–42:**44–46** in. (80–85:**90–95**:100–105:**110–115** cm)
Bust measurement: 34½:**38½**:43:**47½** in. (87.5:**98**:109.5:**120.5** cm)
Length to shoulder: 21:**21½**:22¼:**22½** in. (53:**54.5**:56.5:**57** cm)
Sleeve length: 17:**17**:17½:**17½** in. (43:**43**:44.5:**44.5** cm)

Notes

Charts are read right to left on odd-numbered (RS) rows and left to right on even-numbered (WS) rows.
Strand colors not in use loosely on WS of work.
Labels on charts indicate the starting position for the first use of each Fair Isle panel for each size and pattern piece. When you return to the chart, line up the pattern with the previous panel.

Back

Using MC and US size 2/3 (3 mm) needles, cast on 130:**146**:162:**178** sts.
Row 1 (RS): K2, *p2, k2; rep from * to end.
Row 2: P2, *k2, p2; rep from * to end.
Rep last 2 rows 4 times more, dec one st at center of last row. (129:**145**:161:**177** sts)
Change to US size 3 (3.25 mm) needles.
Beg with a k row work in st st and patt from Chart 1, starting where indicated.
Start Chart 2 where indicated.
Work 2:**2**:4:**4** rows.
Keeping patt correct throughout all charts, dec one st at each end of next row and then on five foll sixth rows. (117:**133**:149:**165** sts)
Start Chart 3 where indicated. Note for sizes 1 and 2 the first row is a dec row, so first and final stitches are worked as k2tog.
Cont dec as set through Chart 3 and Chart 4.
Chart 4 starts where indicated.
Cont to work charts in order throughout Back, keeping patt aligned as set.
When dec are complete (Row 41:**41**:43:**43**), working Chart 1 for second time, work 11:**11**:13:**13** rows cont through charts as set.
Taking inc into patt, inc 1 st at each end of next row and the four foll tenth rows. (127:**143**:159:**175** sts)
Work straight until Back measures 13½:**13½**:13¾:**13¾** in. (34:**34**:34.5:**34.5** cm) from cast-on edge, ending with a WS row.
Make a note on the chart of last row worked.
Shape armholes:
Bind (cast) off 8:**9**:10:**11** sts at beg of next 2 rows. (111:**125**:139:**153** sts)
Dec one st at each end of next 5:**7**:11:**13** rows, then 6:**7**:6:**7** foll RS rows. (89:**97**:105:**113** sts)
Work straight until Back measures 21:**21½**:22¼:**22½** in. (53:**54.5**:56.5:**57** cm) from cast-on edge, ending with a WS row.
Shape shoulders:
Bind (cast) off 12:**14**:15:**16** sts at beg of next 2 rows and 12:**13**:14:**16** sts on foll 2 rows. Leave the rem 41:**43**:47:**49** sts on a spare needle.

Chart 1

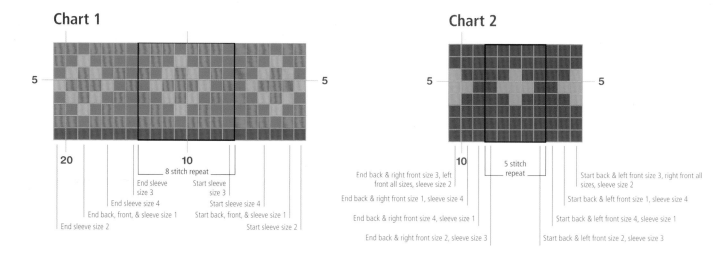

5

5

20

10

8 stitch repeat

End sleeve
size 3

Start sleeve
size 3

End sleeve size 4

Start sleeve size 4

End back, front, & sleeve size 1

Start back, front, & sleeve size 1

End sleeve size 2

Start sleeve size 2

Chart 2

5

5

10

5 stitch
repeat

End back & right front size 3, left
front all sizes, sleeve size 2

Start back & left front size 3, right front all
sizes, sleeve size 2

End back & right front size 1, sleeve size 4

Start back & left front size 1, sleeve size 4

End back & right front size 4, sleeve size 1

Start back & left front size 4, sleeve size 1

End back & right front size 2, sleeve size 3

Start back & left front size 2, sleeve size 3

Chart 3

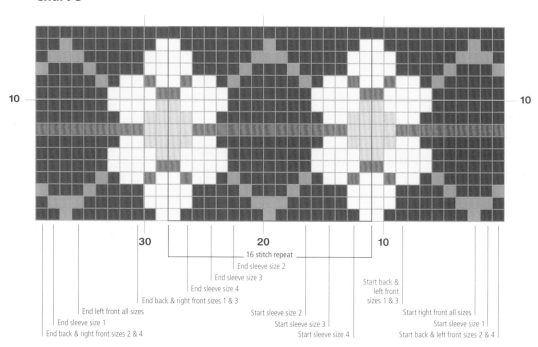

10

10

30

20

10

16 stitch repeat

End sleeve size 2

End sleeve size 3

End sleeve size 4

Start back &
left front
sizes 1 & 3

End back & right front sizes 1 & 3

Start sleeve size 2

End left front all sizes

Start right front all sizes

End sleeve size 1

Start sleeve size 3

Start sleeve size 1

End back & right front sizes 2 & 4

Start sleeve size 4

Start back & left front sizes 2 & 4

Key to colors

- ■ Royal (blue)
- ■ Primrose (yellow)
- ■ Emerald (green)
- ■ Peach Melba (peach)

- ■ Lipstick (deep pink)
- □ Ecru (off-white)
- ■ Candy Pink (pale pink)

Chart 4

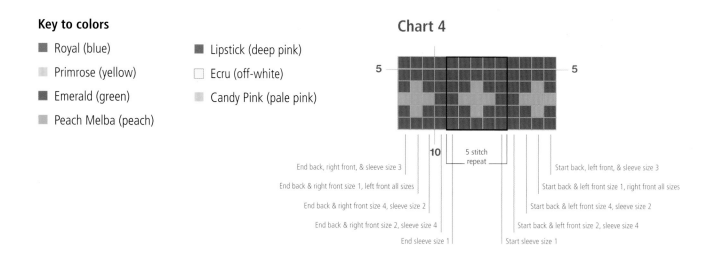

5

5

10

5 stitch
repeat

End back, right front, & sleeve size 3

Start back, left front, & sleeve size 3

End back & right front size 1, left front all sizes

Start back & left front size 1, right front all sizes

End back & right front size 4, sleeve size 2

Start back & left front size 4, sleeve size 2

End back & right front size 2, sleeve size 4

Start back & left front size 2, sleeve size 4

End sleeve size 1

Start sleeve size 1

Left Front

Using MC and US size 2/3 (3 mm) needles, cast on 67:**75**:83:**91** sts.

Row 1 (RS): K2, *p2, k2; rep from * to last st, k1.

Row 2: P3, *k2, p2; rep from * to end.

Rep last 2 rows 4 times more, dec 2 sts across last row.

(65:**73**:81:**89** sts)

Change to US size 3 (3.25 mm) needles.

Beg with a k row, work in st st and patt from Chart 1, starting where indicated.

Start Chart 2 where indicated.

Work 2:**2**:4:**4** rows.

Keeping patt correct throughout all charts, dec one st at beg of next row and then on five foll sixth rows. (59:**67**:75:**83** sts)

Start Chart 3 where indicated. Note for sizes 1 and 2 the first row is a dec row, so first stitch is worked as k2tog.

Cont dec as set through Chart 3 and Chart 4.

Start Chart 4 where indicated.

Cont to work charts in order throughout Front, keeping patt aligned as set.

When dec are complete (Row 41:**41**:43:**43**), working Chart 1 for second time, work 11:**11**:13:**13** rows cont through charts as set. Taking inc into patt, inc 1 st at beg of next and every foll tenth row until there are 64:**72**:80:**88** sts.

Work straight until Front measures 13½:**13½**:13¾:**13¾** in. (34:**34**:34.5:**34.5** cm) from cast-on edge, ending with a WS row.

Shape armhole:

Bind (cast) off 8:**9**:10:**11** sts at beg of next row. (56:**63**:70:**77** sts)

Work 1 row.

Dec one st at armhole edge of the next 5:**7**:11:**13** rows, then 6:**7**:6:**7** foll alt rows. (45:**49**:53:**57** sts.

Work straight until Front measures 17¾:**18¼**:19:**19¼** in. (45:**46.5**:48:**48.5** cm) from cast-on edge, ending with a WS row.

Shape neck:

Next row (RS): Patt 35:**38**:42:**45** sts, turn and leave rem 10:**11**:11:**12** sts on a holder.

Dec one st at neck edge on every row until 24:**27**:29:**32** sts rem. Work straight until Front measures same as Back to shoulder, ending at armhole edge.

Shape shoulder:

Bind (cast) off 12:**14**:15:**16** sts at beg of next row.

Work 1 row.

Bind (cast) off rem 12:**13**:14:**16** sts.

Right Front

Using MC and US size 2/3 (3 mm) needles, cast on 67:**75**:83:**91** sts.

Row 1 (RS): K3, *p2, k2; rep from * to end.

Row 2: P2, *k2, p2; rep from * to last st, p1.

Rep last 2 rows 4 times more, dec 2 sts across last row.

(65:**73**:81:**89** sts)

Change to US size 3 (3.25 mm) needles.

Beg with a k row, work in st st and patt from Chart 1, starting where indicated.

Start Chart 2 where indicated.

Work 2:**2**:4:**4** rows.

Keeping patt correct throughout, dec one st at end of next row and then on five foll sixth rows. (59:**67**:75:**83** sts)

Start Chart 3 where indicated. Note for sizes 1 and 2 the first row is a dec row, so final stitch is worked as k2tog.

Cont dec as set through Chart 3 and Chart 4.

Start Chart 4 where indicated.

Cont to work charts in order throughout Front, keeping patt aligned as set.

When dec are complete (Row 41:**41**:43:**43**), working Chart 1 for second time, work 11:**11**:13:**13** rows cont through charts as set. Taking inc into patt, inc 1 st at beg of next and every foll tenth row until there are 64:**72**:80:**88** sts.

Work straight until Front measures 13½:**13½**:13¾:**13¾** in. (34:**34**:34.5:**34.5** cm) from cast-on edge, ending with a RS row.

Shape armhole:

Bind (cast) off 8:**9**:10:**11** sts at beg of next row. (56:**63**:70:**77** sts)

Dec one st at armhole edge of the next 5:**7**:11:**13** rows, then 6:**7**:6:**7** foll RS rows. (45:**49**:53:**57** sts)

Work straight until Front measures 17¾:**18¼**:19:**19¼** in. (45:**46.5**:48:**48.5** cm) from cast-on edge, ending with a WS row.

Shape neck:

Next row: Patt 10:**11**:11:**12** sts, leave these sts on a holder, patt to end.

Dec one st at neck edge on every row until 24:**27**:29:**32** sts rem. Work straight until Front measures same as Back to shoulder, ending at armhole edge.

Shape shoulder:

Bind (cast) off 12:**14**:15:**16** sts at beg of next row.

Work 1 row.

Bind (cast) off rem 12:**13**:14:**16** sts.

Sleeves

Using MC and US size 2/3 (3 mm) needles, cast on 58:**62**:66:**70** sts.

Row 1 (RS): K2, *p2, k2; rep from * to end.

Row 2: P2, *k2, p2; rep from * to end.

Rep last 2 rows 12 times more, inc one st at center of last row. (59:**63**:67:**71** sts)

Change to US size 3 (3.25 mm) needles.

Beg with a k row, work in st st and stripes of 2 rows each of MC, A, MC, B, MC, C, MC, D, and MC **at the same time**, inc one st at each end of third and two foll sixth rows. (65:**69**:73:**77** sts)

Cont in patt from Chart 1, starting where indicated.

Work 2 rows.

Inc and work into patt one st at each end of the next and every foll sixth row until there are 97:**103**:109:**113** sts.

Cont with shaping throughout rep of Charts 1 to 4 as for body, starting pattern rep as indicated on charts.

Work straight until Sleeve measures approx. 17¼:**17¼**:17¾:**17¾** in. (43.5:**43.5**:45:**45** cm) from cast-on edge, ending with same WS marked chart row as for Back.

Shape top:

Bind (cast) off 8:**9**:10:**11** sts at beg of next 2 rows. (81:**85**:89:**91** sts)

Dec one st at each end of the next 5:**7**:9:**11** rows.

Dec on st each end of 13:**13**:13:**13** foll RS rows. (45:**45**:45:**63** sts)

Size 4 only:

Dec one st at each end of every foll fourth row until 59 sts rem, then dec one st at each end of next five RS rows. (–:–:–:**49** sts)

All sizes:

Dec one st at each end of foll 5:**5**:5:**7** rows. (35 sts)

Bind (cast) off 6 sts at beg of next 4 rows.

Bind (cast) off rem 11 sts.

Neckband

Join shoulder seams.

With RS facing and using MC and US size 2/3 (3 mm) needles, slip 10:**11**:11:**12** sts from Right Front neck holder onto a needle, pick up and k 29 sts up Right Front neck, k41:**43**:47:**49** sts from Back neck holder, pick up and k 30 sts down Left Front neck, then k10:**11**:11:**12** sts from Left Front holder. (120:**124**:128:**132** sts)

Rib row 1 (WS): P3, *k2, p2: rep from * to last 5 sts, k2, p3.

Rib row 2: K3, *p2, k2; rep from * to last 5 sts, p2, k3.

Rep the last 2 rows twice more and then Row 1 again.

Bind (cast) off in rib.

top tip

This is a very busy Fair Isle design. Use a stitch marker to keep track of where you are on the pattern or mark off each row on the charts as you go.

Button Band

With RS facing, using MC and US size 2/3 (3 mm) needles, pick up and k 110:**114**:118:**122** sts evenly along Left Front edge.

Rib row 1 (WS): P2, *k2, p2; rep from * to end.

Rib row 2: K2, *p2, k2; rep from * to end.

Rep last 2 rows twice more and then Row 1 again.

Bind (cast) off in rib.

Buttonhole Band

With RS facing, using MC and US size 2/3 (3 mm) needles, pick up and k 110:**114**:118:**122** sts evenly along Right Front edge.

Rib row 1 (WS): P2, *k2, p2; rep from * to end.

Rib row 2: K2, *p2, k2; rep from * to end.

Rib row 3: As Rib row 1.

Buttonhole row: Rib 3:**5**:3:**5**, yrn, rib 2tog [rib 11:**11**:12:**12**, yrn, rib 2tog] 8 times, rib 1:**3**:1:**3**.

Rib 3 more rows.

Bind (cast) off in rib.

Finishing

Join side and sleeve seams using mattress stitch carefully matching patt. Sew sleeves into armholes, matching patt and easing to fit. Sew on buttons to match buttonhole positions.

retro vest top

This vest top is a gorgeous item and is definitely on trend. It's not only fashionable but also warm, and the colors work beautifully together.

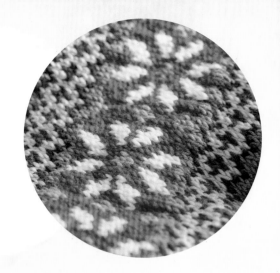

materials

- Debbie Bliss Rialto DK (100% extra-fine merino wool) light worsted (DK) yarn
    - 4:**5**:5:**6**:6:**6**:7:**7**:8 x 1¾ oz (50 g) balls – approx. 115 yd (105 m) per ball – of shade 45 Gold (A)
    - 1:**1**:1:**2**:2:**2**:2:**2**:2 x 1¾ oz (50 g) balls – approx. 115 yd (105 m) per ball – of shade 40 Purple (B)
    - ½:**½**:½:**½**:½:**¾**:¾:**¾**:¾ x 1¾ oz (50 g) ball – approx. 58/87 yd (53/80 m) per ball – of shade 02 Ecru (off-white) (C)
    - 1:**1**:2:**2**:2:**2**:2:**2**:2 x 1¾ oz (50 g) balls – approx. 115 yd (105 m) per ball – of shade 34 Fuchsia (bright pink) (D)
    - ¼ x 1¾oz (50 g) ball – approx. 29 yd (26 m) – of shade 44 Aqua (blue) (E)
    - ½:**½**:½:**½**:½:**¾**:¾:**¾**:¾ x 1¾ oz (50 g) ball – approx. 58/87 yd (53/80 m) – of shade 42 Pink (pale pink) (F)
    - ½ x 1¾oz (50 g) ball – approx. 58 yd (53 m) – of shade 53 Basil (green) (G)
- US size 3 (3.25 mm) and US size 6 (4 mm) knitting needles
- Safety pin
- Stitch holder
- Yarn sewing needle

gauge (tension)

25 sts and 27 rows over 4 in. (10 cm) square working Fair Isle patt in st st on US size 6 (4 mm) needles.
22 sts and 30 rows over 4 in. (10 cm) square in st st on US size 6 (4 mm) needles.

finished size

Women's sizes: 1:**2**:3:**4**:5
To fit size: 32:**34**:36:**38**:40 in. (80:**85**:90:**95**:100 cm)
Bust measurement: 34:**36¼**:38¼:**40½**:42½ in. (86:**92**:97:**103**:108 cm)
Length: 19¾:**20**:20½:**21¼**:21¾ in. (50:**51**:52:**54**:55 cm)

Men's sizes: **6**:7:**8**:9
To fit size: **44**:46:**48**:50 in. (**110**:115:**120**:125 cm)
Bust measurement: **45**:47:**49**:51 in. (**112.5**:117.5:**122.5**:127.5 cm)
Length: **24**:25:**25**:26 in. (**60**:62.5:**62.5**:65 cm)

Notes

Chart is read right to left on odd-numbered (RS) rows and left to right on even-numbered (WS) rows.
Strand colors not in use loosely on WS of work.

Front

Using US size 3 (3.25 mm) needles and B, cast on 85:**91**:97:**105**:111:**119**:125:**129**:135 sts.
Row 1 (RS): K1, *p1, k1 rib; rep from * to end.
Row 2 (WS): P1, *k1, p1 rib; rep from * to end.
Change to A and rep these 2 rows for 2 in. (5 cm), ending on RS row.
Next row (WS): Rib 4:**6**:9:**8**:6:**10**:7:**6**:9 sts, M1, *rib 7:**6**:6:**8**:9:**9**:10:**9**:9, M1; rep from * to last 4:**7**:10:**9**:6:**10**:8:**6**:9 sts, rib to end. (97:**105**:111:**117**:123:**131**:137:**143**:149 sts)
Change to US size 6 (4 mm) needles.
Starting with a k row, work in st st until work measures 5:**5½**:5½:**6**:6:**7¼**:7½:**7½**:8 in. (13:**14**:14:**15**:15:**18**:19:**19**:20 cm), ending on a RS row.
Next row: p3:**3**:6:**3**:1:**5**:8:**5**:3, *M1, p10:**11**:11:**10**:11:**11**:11:**11**:12:11; rep from * to last 4:**3**:6:**4**:1:**5**:8:**6**:3 sts, M1, p4:**3**:6:**4**:1:**5**:8:**6**:3. (107:**115**:121:**129**:135:**143**:149:**155**:163 sts)

Beg with a k row and joining in colors as required, cont in st st working Chart 1, starting and ending as indicated.

Work Chart 2, starting and ending as indicated.

Work Chart 3, starting and ending as indicated.

Row 13 of Chart 3: K3:**2**:1:**3**:0:**4**:7:**5**:2, *k2tog, k9:**10**:11:**9**:10:**10**:10:**11**:10, rep from * to last 5:**5**:5:**3**:5:**3**:7:**10**:7:5 sts, k2tog k3:**3**:1:**3**:1:**5**:8:**5**:3. (97:**105**:111:**117**:123:**131**:137:**143**:149 sts)

Complete Chart 3 and cont in A only.

Shape armholes:

Bind (cast) off 4:**4**:5:**5**:6:**6**:7:**7**:8 sts at beg of next 2 rows. (89:**97**:101:**107**:111:**119**:123:**129**:133 sts)

Dec 1 st at each end of next 5:**5**:5:**7**:9:**9**:9:**11**:11 rows, then on foll 5:**5**:5:**6**:5:**5**:5:**5**:5 alt rows. (69:**77**:81:**81**:83:**91**:95:**97**:101 sts)

Divide for neck:

Next row (RS): Dec 1 st, patt until there are33:**37**:39:**39**:40:**44**:46:**47**:49 sts on right-hand needle, turn and complete this side first. Work 1 row.

Next row: Dec 1 st at armhole, work to last 2 sts before neck edge, k2tog. (31:**35**:37:**37**:38:**42**:44:**45**:47 sts)

Keeping armhole straight, cont to dec 1 st at neck edge on every alt row until 23:**24**:26:**27**:28:**30**:32:**32**:32 sts rem, then on every 4th row until 19:**20**:21:**21**:22:**24**:25:**25**:26 sts rem.

Work straight until armhole measures 7¾:**8¼**:8¼:**8¾**:9:**10**:10¼:**10½**:11 in. (20:**21**:21:**22**:23:**25**:26:**26.5**:27.5 cm) from start, ending with WS row.

Shape shoulder:

Bind (cast) off 6:**7**:7:**7**:7:**8**:8:**8**:9 sts at beg of next and foll alt row.

Work 1 row.

Bind (cast) off rem 7:**6**:7:**7**:8:**8**:9:**9**:8 sts.

With RS facing, slip center st onto a safety pin. Rejoin yarn to rem sts and k to last 2 sts, k2tog. (33:**37**:37:**39**:40:**44**:46:**47**:49 sts)

Complete to match first side of neck, reversing shapings.

Back

Work as for Front to beg of neck shaping.

Dec one st each end of every alt row to 65:**73**:77:**77**:79:**87**:91:**93**:97 sts.

Cont straight in patt until armhole matches Front to shoulder shaping.

Shape shoulders:

Bind (cast) off 6:**7**:7:**7**:7:**8**:8:**8**:9 sts at beg of next 4 rows, then 7:**6**:7:**7**:8:**8**:9:**9**:8 sts on next 2 rows.

Cut yarn and leave rem 27:**33**:35:**35**:35:**39**:41:**43**:45 sts on st holder.

Neck border

Join right shoulder seam with mattress st.

With RS facing and using US size 3 (3.25 mm) needles and A, pick up and k 38:**40**:42:**42**:44:**48**:50:**50**:52 sts down left front neck, place marker, k1 from safety pin, pick up and k 38:**40**:42:**42**:44:**48**:50:**50**:52 sts up right front neck, then k across 27:**33**:35:**35**:35:**39**:41:**43**:45 sts from st holder, inc1 at center back. (105:**115**:121:**121**:125:**137**:143:**145**:151 sts.

Row 1 (WS): *P1, k1; rep from * until 1 st before marker, p1, slip marker, **k1, p1; rep from ** to end.

Row 2 (RS): *K1, p1; rep from * until 3 sts before marker, p1, ssk, slip marker, k1, k2tog, **p1, k1; rep from ** to end.

Row 3 (WS): *P1, k1; rep from * until 4 sts before marker, p1, k2tog, p1, slip marker, ssk, p1, **k1, p1; rep from ** to end.

Rep last 2 rows once more.

Change to B and work Rows 2–3 once more.

Bind (cast) off in rib, dec on each side of center st as set.

Armhole borders

Join left shoulder and neck border seam with mattress st.

With RS facing and using US size 3 (3.25 mm) needles and A, pick up and k 107:**109**:113:**117**:121:**130**:136:**140**:144 sts evenly around armhole edge.

Beg with second row, work in rib as given for Front for 5 rows.

Change to B and work 2 more rows in rib.

Bind (cast) off in rib.

Finishing

Press carefully according to directions on ball band and join side seams using mattress st.

Chart 1

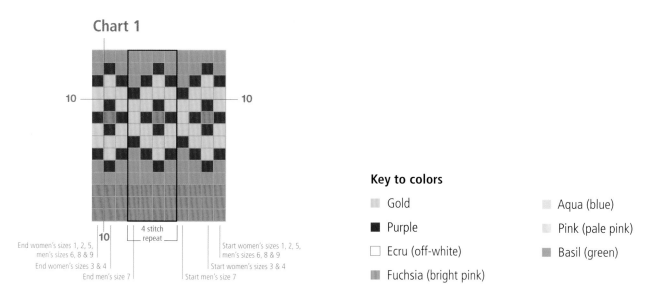

10

10

10

4 stitch repeat

End women's sizes 1, 2, 5,
men's sizes 6, 8 & 9

End women's sizes 3 & 4

End men's size 7

Start women's sizes 1, 2, 5,
men's sizes 6, 8 & 9

Start women's sizes 3 & 4

Start men's size 7

Key to colors

Gold

Purple

Ecru (off-white)

Fuchsia (bright pink)

Aqua (blue)

Pink (pale pink)

Basil (green)

Chart 2

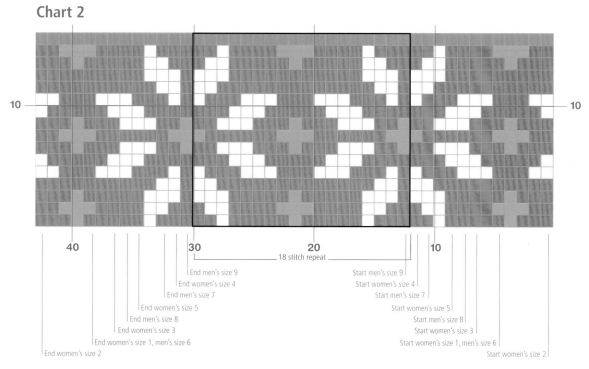

10

10

40

30

20

18 stitch repeat

10

End men's size 9

End women's size 4

End men's size 7

End women's size 5

End men's size 8

End women's size 3

End women's size 1, men's size 6

End women's size 2

Start men's size 9

Start women's size 4

Start men's size 7

Start women's size 5

Start men's size 8

Start women's size 3

Start women's size 1, men's size 6

Start women's size 2

Chart 3

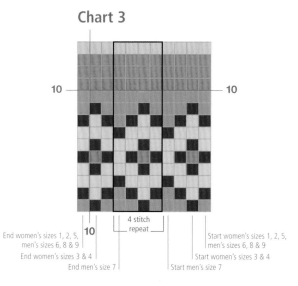

10

10

10

10

4 stitch repeat

End women's sizes 1, 2, 5,
men's sizes 6, 8 & 9

End women's sizes 3 & 4

End men's size 7

Start women's sizes 1, 2, 5,
men's sizes 6, 8 & 9

Start women's sizes 3 & 4

Start men's size 7

brights and tweed sweater

Fair Isle can get a little lost in tweed, but the lovely bright colors in this sweater work well and make it look contemporary and stunning.

materials

- Debbie Bliss Donegal Luxury Tweed Aran (90% wool/10% angora) worsted (aran) yarn
    7:**7**:8:**9**:10 x 1¾ oz (50 g) balls – approx. 96.5 yd (88 m) per ball – of shade 10 Silver (pale gray) (MC)
    1:**1**:1:**1**:1 x 1¾ oz (50 g) ball – approx. 96.5 yd (88 m) – each of shades 07 Oatmeal (off-white), 21 Fuchsia (pink), 37 Tangerine (orange-red), 36 Gold (yellow), 38 Rose Pink (mid pink)
- US size 4 (3.5 mm) and US size 7 (4.5 mm) circular needles
- US size 4 (3.5 mm) and US size 7 (4.5 mm) double-pointed needles
- Yarn sewing needle

gauge (tension)

18 sts x 24 rows over 4 in. (10 cm) square working st st using US size 7 (4.5 mm) needles.

finished size

To fit size: 32:**34**:36:**38**:40 in. (80:**85**:90:**95**:100 cm)
Bust measurement: 32¾:**35½**:38¼:**42**:44½ in. (83:**90**:97:**107**:113 cm)
Length to shoulder: 22:**22½**:23¼:**24**:24¾ in. (56:**57**:59:**61**:63 cm)

Notes

Chart is read right to left on every row.
Strand colors not in use loosely on WS of work.

Body

Using MC and US size 4 (3.5 mm) circular needle, cast on 150:**162**:174:**192**:204 sts. Join in a circle and work (k1, p1) rib for 1½ in. (4 cm).
Change to US size 7 (4.5 mm) circular needle and work 2 rows in st st.
Work patt from Chart 1 in st st.
When patt is complete, cont with MC until body measures 14½:**15**:15¾:**16½**:17¼ in. (37:**38**:40:**42**:44 cm) from cast-on edge.
Next row: Bind (cast) off 4:**5**:6:**7**:8 sts, k67:**71**:75:**82**:86 sts including st on RH needle after bind (cast) off, bind (cast) off 8:**10**:12:**14**:16 sts, k67:**71**:75:**82**:86 sts including st on RH needle after bind (cast) off, bind (cast) off 4:**5**:6:**7**:8 sts.
Fasten off. (134:**142**:150:**164**:176 sts)
Set aside and work sleeves.

Sleeves

(make 2)
Using MC and US size 4 (3.5 mm) dpns, cast on 36:**42**:42:**48**:48 sts.
Join in a circle and work (k1, p1) rib for 1½ in. (4 cm).
Change to US size 7 (4.5 mm) dpns and work 2 rows in st st.
Work patt from Chart 1 in st st.
When patt is finished, cont with MC.
Inc 1 st after first st and 1 st before last st of round on next and every 7th:**9th**:7th:**9th**:7th round to 56:**60**:64:**68**:72 sts.
Work straight until Sleeve measures 16¾:**17**:17⅛:**17¼**:17½ in. (42.5:**43**:43.5:**44**:44.5 cm).
Bind (cast) off 4:**5**:6:**7**:8 sts, k to last 4:**5**:6:**7**:8 sts, bind (cast) off. (48:**50**:52:**54**:56 sts)

Yoke

Join body and sleeves:
Using MC and US size 7 (4.5 mm) circular needle, k sts from first Sleeve then from front, second Sleeve and back. (230:**242**:254:**272**:284 sts)

Start to work from Chart 2 (dec as indicated below).

Round 4: [K7:**6**:6:**7**:7, k2tog] 6:**5**:8:**4**:7 times, [k6:**5**:5:**6**:6, k2tog] 2:**7**:1:**8**:2 times, [k7:**6**:6:**7**:7, k2tog] 11:**9**:15:**8**:14 times, [k6:**5**:5:**6**:6, k2tog] 2:**7**:1:**8**:2 times, [k7:**6**:6:**7**:7, k2tog] 5:**4**:7:**4**:7 times. (204:**210**:222:**240**:252 sts)

Round 14: [K6:**7**:6:**6**:5, k2tog] 2:**1**:3:**4**:36 times, [k5:**6**:5:**5**:0, k2tog] 10:**12**:9:**8**:0 times, [k6:**7**:6:**6**:0, k2tog] 4:**1**:6:**8**:0 times, [k5:**6**:5:**5**:0, k2tog] 10:**12**:9:**8**:0 times, [k6:**0**:6:**6**:0, k2tog] 2:**0**:3:**4**:0 times. (176:**184**:192:**208**:216 sts)

Now work Chart 3.

Round 15: [K4:**7**:5:**6**:4, k2tog] 4:**2**:3:**3**:36 times, [k3:**6**:4:**5**:0, k2tog] 8:**7**:9:**8**:0 times, [k4:**7**:5:**6**:0, k2tog] 8:**4**:6:**6**:0 times, [k3:**6**:4:**5**:0, k2tog] 8:**7**:9:**8**:0 times, [k4:**7**:5:**6**:0, k2tog] 4:**2**:3:**3**:0 times. (144:**162**:162:**180**:180 sts)

Now work Chart 4.

Round 10: [K2:**2**:2:**2**:2, k2tog] 36:**19**:19:**45**:45 times, [k-:**3**:3:**0**:0, k2tog] 0:**2**:2:**0**:0 times, [k0:**2**:2:**0**:0, k2tog] 0:**19**:19:**0**:0 times. (108:**122**:122:**135**:135 sts)

Round 13: [K4:**2**:4:**2**:5, k2tog] 2:**7**:1:**4**:2 times, [k3:**1**:3:**3**:4, k2tog] 6:**3**:11:**7**:6 times, [k4:**2**:4:**9**:5, k2tog] 4:**13**:1:**3**:5 times, [k3:**1**:3:**3**:4, k2tog] 6:**3**:11:**7**:6 times, [k4:**2**:-:**2**:5, k2tog] 2:**6**:0:**4**:2 times. (88:**90**:98:**110**:114 sts)

Neckband:

Change to US size 4 (3.5 mm) circular needles and cont in MC. Work 2:**2**:2:**1**:1 rounds.

Next round: [K0:**0**:0:**26**:27, k2tog] 0:**0**:0:**1**:1 time, [k0:**0**:0:**25**:26, k2tog] 0:**0**:0:**1**:1 time, [k0:**0**:0:**26**:27, k2tog] 0:**0**:0:**1**:1 time, [k0:**0**:0:**25**:26, k2tog] 0:**0**:0:**1**:1 time. (88:**90**:98:**106**:110 sts)

Work (k1, p1) rib for 3¼ in. (8 cm).

Bind (cast) off loosely.

Finishing

Sew underarm bound (cast) off edges together, and weave in loose ends. Fold neckband in half to outside and slipstitch in place.

Key to colors

- ■ Silver (pale gray)
- □ Oatmeal (off-white)
- ■ Fuchsia (pink)
- ■ Tangerine (orange-red)
- ■ Gold (yellow)
- ■ Rose Pink (mid pink)

Chart 1

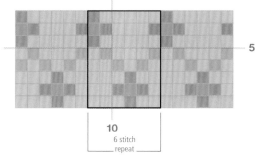

5

10
6 stitch
repeat

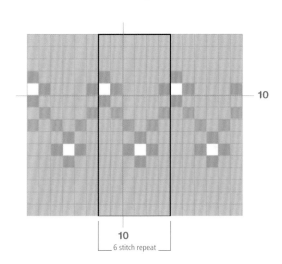

Chart 2

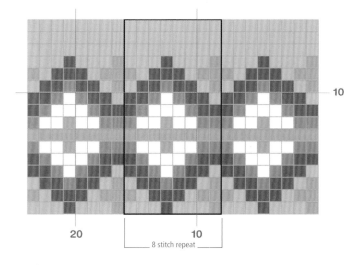

10

20   10
8 stitch repeat

Chart 3

10

10
6 stitch repeat

Chart 4

10

30   20   10
16 stitch repeat

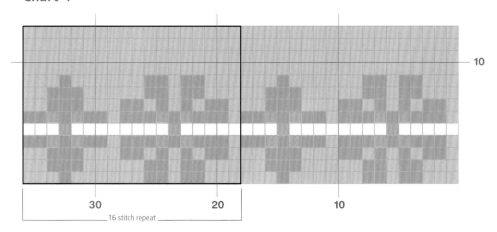

vintage-style cardigan

I was inspired by some vintage patterns when I was designing this and then I found some interesting traditional Fair Isle patterns to add, which I worked in more contemporary colors.

materials

- Debbie Bliss Baby Cashmerino (55% merino wool/33% microfiber/12% cashmere) light worsted (DK) yarn
    3:**3**:4:**4** x 1¾ oz (50 g) balls – approx. 137 yd (125 m) per ball – of shade 059 Mallard (dark blue) (A)
    7:**7**:8:**9** x 1¾ oz (50 g) balls – approx. 137 yd (125 m) per ball – of shade 101 Ecru (off-white) (B)
    2:**2**:3:**3** x 1¾ oz (50 g) balls – approx. 137 yd (125 m) per ball – of shade 067 Sienna (orange) (C)
    2:**2**:2:**2** x 1¾ oz (50 g) balls – approx. 137 yd (125 m) per ball – of shade 202 Light Blue (E)
- US size 2 (2.75 mm) and US size 3 (3.25 mm) knitting needles
- Yarn sewing needle
- 9 buttons

gauge (tension)

27 sts x 34 rows over 4 in. (10 cm) square working Fair Isle patt in st st using US size 3 (3.25 mm) needles.

finished size

To fit: 32–34:**36**–**38**:40–42:**44**–**46** in. (82–87:**92**–**97**:102–107: **112**–**117** cm)
Bust measurement: 36:**39½**:46:**49½** in. (91:**100**:117:**126** cm)
Length to shoulder: 19¾:**20**:20½:**21** in. (50:**51**:52:**53** cm)
Sleeve length: 18½ in. (47 cm)

Notes

Charts are read right to left on odd-numbered (RS) rows and left to right on even-numbered (WS) rows.

Back

Using A and US size 2 (2.75 mm) needles, cast on 123:**135**:159: **171** sts.
Row 1: K1, [p1, k1] to end.
Row 2: P1, [k1, p1] to end.
Rep the last 2 rows 8 times more.
Change to US size 3 (3.25 mm) needles.
Beg with a k row, cont in st st.
Work 2 rows.
Cont in patt from Chart.
Chart row 1: Starting where indicated work across Chart, working 24-st patt rep 5:**5**:6:**7** times, finishing where indicated.
Cont in patt to end of row 54.
Now rep Rows 49–54 until Back measures 11¾:**11¾**:12¼:**12¼** in. (30:**30**:31:**31** cm) from cast-on edge, ending with a WS row.
Shape armholes:
Using B, bind (cast) off 7:**9**:13:**15** sts at beg of next 2 rows keeping patt correct for rest of rows. (109:**117**:133:**141** sts)
Dec one st at each end of the next 5:**7**:11:**13** rows then 5:**3**:3:**1** foll RS rows. (89:**97**:105:**113** sts)
Work straight until Back measures 19¾:**20**:20½:**21** in. (50:**51**:52:**53** cm) from cast-on edge, ending with a WS row.
Shape shoulders:
Bind (cast) off 12:**14**:15:**16** sts at beg of next 2 rows and 13:**14**:15:**17** sts on foll 2 rows.
Leave the rem 39:**41**:45:**47** sts on a spare needle.

Left Front

Using A and US size 2 (2.75 mm) needles, cast on 63:**69**:81:**87** sts.

Row 1: P1, [k1, p1] to end.

Row 2: K1, [p1, k1] to end.

Rep the last 2 rows 8 times more.

Change to US size 3 (3.25 mm) needles.

Beg with a k row, cont in st st.

Work 2 rows.

Cont in patt from Chart.

Chart row 1: Starting where indicated work across Chart, working 24-st patt rep 2:**2**:3:**3** times and finishing where indicated.

Cont in patt to end of Row 54.

Now rep Rows 49–54 until Front measures 11¾:**11¾**:12¼:**12¼** in. (30:**30**:31:**31** cm) from cast-on edge, ending with a WS row.

Shape armhole:

Using B bind (cast) off 7:**9**:13:**15** sts at beg of next row, keeping patt correct for rest of rows. (56:**60**:68:**72** sts)

Work 1 row.

Dec one st at armhole edge of the next 5:**7**:11:**13** rows, then 5:**3**:3:**1** foll RS rows. (46:**50**:54:**58** sts)

Work straight until Front measures 17:**17½**:17¾:**18** in. (43:**44**:44.5:**45.5** cm) from cast-on edge, ending with a WS row.

Shape neck:

Next row: Patt to last 12:**13**:14:**15** sts, turn, leaving rem sts on a holder.

Dec one st at neck edge on every row until 25:**28**:30:**33** sts rem.

Work straight until Front measures same as Back to shoulder shaping, ending at armhole edge.

Shape shoulder:

Bind (cast) off 12:**14**:15:**16** sts at beg of next row.

Work 1 row.

Bind (cast) off rem 13:**14**:15:**17** sts.

Right Front

Using A and US size 2 (2.75 mm) needles, cast on 63:**69**:81:**87** sts.

Row 1: P1, [k1, p1] to end.

Row 2: K1, [p1, k1] to end.

Rep the last 2 rows 8 times more.

Change to US size 3 (3.25 mm) needles.

Beg with a k row, cont in st st.

Work 2 rows.

Cont in patt from Chart.

Chart row 1: Starting where indicated work across Chart, working 24-st patt rep 2:**2**:3:**3** times and finishing where indicated.

Cont in patt to end of Row 54.

Now rep Rows 49–54 until Front measures 11¾:**11¾**:12¼:**12¼** in. (30:**30**:31:**31** cm) from cast-on edge, ending with a RS row.

Shape armhole:

Using B, bind (cast) off 7:**9**:13:**15** sts at beg of next row, keeping

patt correct for rest of rows. (56:**60**:68:**72** sts)

Dec one st at armhole edge of next 5:**7**:11:**13** rows, then 5:**3**:3:**1** foll RS rows. (46:**50**:54:**58** sts)

Work straight until Front measures 17:**17½**:17¾:**18** in. (43:**44**:44.5:**45.5** cm) from cast-on edge, ending with a WS row.

Shape neck:

Next row: Using A k12:**13**:14:**15** sts, leave these sts on a holder, patt to end.

Dec one st at neck edge on every row until 25:**28**:30:**33** sts rem.

Work straight until Front measures same as Back to shoulder shaping, ending at armhole edge.

Shape shoulder:

Bind (cast) off 12:**14**:15:**16** sts at beg of next row.

Work 1 row.

Bind (cast) off rem 13:**14**:15:**17** sts.

Sleeves

Using A and US size 2 (2.75 mm) needles, cast on 51:**57**:69:**75** sts.

Row 1: P1, [k1, p1] to end.

Row 2: K1, [p1, k1] to end.

Rep the last 2 rows 8 times more.

Change to US size 3 (3.25 mm) needles.

Beg with a k row, cont in st st.

Work 2 rows.

Cont in patt from Chart.

Chart row 1: Starting where indicated work across Chart, working 24-st patt rep 2:**2**:2:**3** times and finishing where indicated.

Cont in patt to end of Row 36.

Rep Rows 31–36 to form main patt, **at the same time** inc 1 st at each end of Chart row 3, working into patt, and then every foll sixth row until there are 95:**101**:113:**119** sts.

Work straight until Sleeve measures approx. 18½ in. (47 cm) from cast-on edge, ending with the same patt row as Back to armhole shaping.

Shape top:

Using B, bind (cast) off 7:**9**:13:**15** sts at beg of next 2 rows, keeping patt correct for rest of rows. (81:**83**:87:**89** sts)

Dec 1 st at each end of next and 15:**16**:12:**15** foll alt rows. (49:**49**:61:**57** sts)

Dec 1 st at each end of every row to 35 sts.

Bind (cast) off 6 sts at beg of next 4 rows.

Bind (cast) off.

Neckband

Join shoulder seams.

With RS facing, using A and US size 2 (2.75 mm) needles, k12:**13**:14:**15** sts from Right Front neck holder, pick up and k 20:**20**:21:**21** sts up Right Front neck, k39:**41**:45:**47** sts from Back neck holder, pick up and k 20:**20**:21:**21** sts down Left Front neck,

then k12:**13**:14:**15** sts from Left Front holder. (103:**107**:115:**119** sts)
Row 1: P1, [k1, p1] to end.
Row 2: K1, [p1, k1] to end.
Rep last 2 rows once more.
Bind (cast) off in rib.

Button Band
With RS facing, using A and US size 2 (2.75 mm) needles, pick up and k 137:**145**:149:**153** sts along Left Front edge.
Row 1: P1, [k1, p1] to end.
Row 2: K1, [p1, k1] to end.
Rep last 2 rows once more.
Bind (cast) off in rib.

Buttonhole Band
With RS facing, using A and US size 2 (2.75 mm) needles, pick up and k 137:**145**:149:**153** sts along Right Front edge.
Row 1: P1, [k1, p1] to end.
This row sets the rib
Buttonhole row: Rib 3, yrn, rib 2tog, [rib 14:**15**:15:**16**, yrn, rib

2tog, rib 14:**15**:16:**16**, yrn, rib 2tog] 4 times, rib 4.
Rib 2 rows.
Bind (cast) off in rib.

Collar
Using A and US size 2 (2.75 mm) needles, cast on 121:**125**:129:**133** sts.
Row 1: K.
Row 2: K12, s2 k1 psso, k to last 15 sts, s2 k1 psso, k12.
Row 3: P to end.
Row 4: K11, s2 k1 psso, k to last 14 sts, s2 k1 psso, k11.
Row 5: P to end.
Row 6: K10, s2 k1 psso, k to last 13 sts, s2 k1 psso, k10.
Row 7: P to end.
Cont in this way until foll row has been worked: K1, s2 k1 psso, k to last 4 sts, s2 k1 psso, k1. (73:**77**:81:**85** sts)
Next row: P to end.
Bind (cast) off 5 sts at beg of next 8:**8**:10:**10** rows. (33:**37**:31:**35** sts)
Bind (cast) off.

Key to colors

■ Mallard (dark blue) ■ Sienna (orange)

□ Ecru (off-white) ■ Light Blue

Chart 1

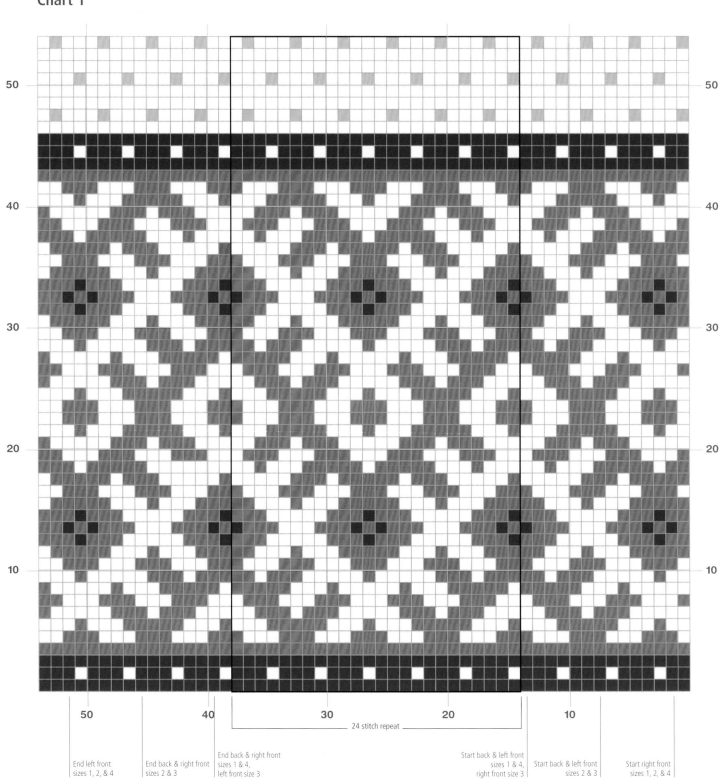

24 stitch repeat

| End left front sizes 1, 2, & 4 | End back & right front sizes 2 & 3 | End back & right front sizes 1 & 4, left front size 3 | Start back & left front sizes 1 & 4, right front size 3 | Start back & left front sizes 2 & 3 | Start right front sizes 1, 2, & 4 |

Finishing

Join side and sleeve seams using mattress stitch, and sew in sleeves.

Lightly steam collar to flatten edge and join round neckband, ensuring that RS of collar is outward when collar is folded back. Ease to fit and leave front bands free. Sew on buttons to match buttonhole positions. Press button bands and sew around edge of collar to keep in place on cardigan.

Chart 2

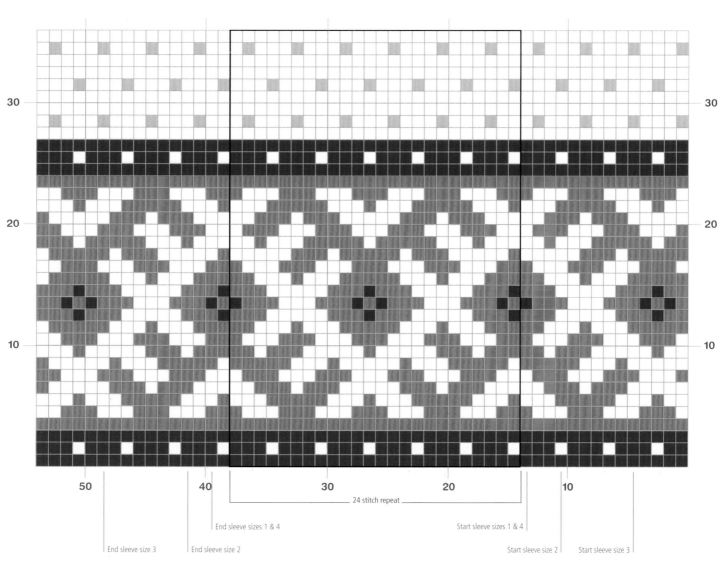

CHAPTER 2
accessories

fair isle bobble hat

I couldn't resist putting a really big bobble on this hat!
The design works well for a man or a woman and it's a bit
of a showstopper.

materials

- Debbie Bliss Rialto Chunky (100% extra-fine merino wool) bulky
  (chunky) weight yarn
  - 2 x 1¾ oz (50 g) balls – approx. 66 yd (60 m) per ball – of shade
    03 Ecru (off-white) (A)
  - ½ x 1¾ oz (50 g) ball – approx. 33 yd (30 m) – each of shades
    17 Lime (green) (B), 19 Aqua (blue) (C)
  - 1 x 1¾ oz (50 g) ball – approx. 66 yd (60 m) – of shade 15 Ruby
    (red) (D)
- US size 10½ (6.5 mm) double-pointed needles
- US size 10 (6 mm) circular needle, length 24 in. (60 cm)
- Stitch marker
- Yarn sewing needle

gauge (tension)

15 sts and 21 rows over 4 in. (10 cm) square working st st using
US size 10 (6 mm) needles.

finished size

To fit an average size woman's head

special technique

Magic loop
Cast on sts and divide in half equally, placing half on one needle
and rem on cord. Pull a length of cord through gap between two
sets of sts, ensuring row is not twisted. Join for working in the
round by placing a st marker for first st of round, pull RH needle
slightly out of its sts, while leaving other half of sts on LH needle.
Knit sts from LH needle as usual, using RH needle, pulling tightly on
yarn for first couple of sts to ensure round joins seamlessly.
The RH needle will now have sts on it and the LH needle will not.
Pull cord so sts move to LH needle and then pull out RH needle,
leaving its sts on cord, so you can use it to knit off LH needle. Cont
in this way for required length.

Notes
Chart is read right to left on every row.
Strand colors not in use loosely on WS of work.

Chart 1

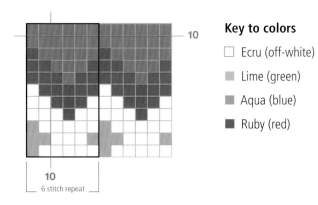

10

10
6 stitch repeat

Key to colors

☐ Ecru (off-white)

☐ Lime (green)

☐ Aqua (blue)

☐ Ruby (red)

Chart 2

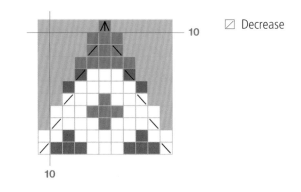

10

☑ Decrease

10

Hat

Using US size 10 (6 mm) circular needle and A, cast on 78 sts. Make a magic loop (see special technique on page 48) to join and place st marker.

Brim:

Round 1: [K1, p1] rib to end.

Rep Round 1 until work measures 1½ in. (4 cm).

Cont in A and st st until work measures 3 in. (7.5 cm) from cast-on edge.

Follow rounds 1–11 from Chart 1, reading Chart from bottom and rows from right to left.

Change to US size 10½ (6.5 mm) dpns.

Crown:

Follow Chart 2, making dec in places shown on chart. Alternatively, follow written instructions below:

Shaping:

Round 12 (dec row): *k2tog tbl in A, k3 in D, k3 in A, k3 in D, k2tog in A; rep from * to end. (66 sts)

Round 13: *K2 in A, k1 in D, k5 in A, k1 in D, k2 in A; rep from * to end.

Round 14 (dec row): *K2tog tbl in A, k3 in A, k1 in C, k3 in A, k2tog in A; rep from * to end. (54 sts)

Round 15: *K3 in A, k3 in C, k3 in A; rep from * to end.

Round 16 (dec row): *K2tog tbl in A, k2 in A, k1 in C, k2 in A, k2tog in A; rep from * to end. (42 sts)

Round 17: *K1 in D, k5 in A, k1 in D; rep from * to end.

Round 18 (dec row): *K2tog tbl in D, k3 in A, k2tog in D; rep from * to end. (30 sts)

Round 19: Using C, knit to end.

Round 20 (dec row): Using C, *k2tog tbl, k1, k2tog; rep from * to end. (18 sts)

Round 21: Using C, knit to end.

Round 22: Using C, *s2 k1 psso; rep from * to end. (6 sts)

Break yarn, leaving a long tail. Thread a yarn sewing needle with tail and thread through last 6 sts and pull tight to close gap.

Finishing

Using all colors, make a large loose pompom (see page 62) approx. 6 in. (15 cm) in diameter and attach to top of hat.

fair isle neck warmer

This is a small but beautiful cowl, designed to just tuck under the chin and round the neck underneath a coat. Perfect for chilly days.

materials

- Debbie Bliss Rialto 4-ply (100% extra-fine merino wool) fingering (4-ply) yarn

    1 x 1¾ oz (50 g) ball – approx. 197 yd (180 m) – of shade 27 Silver (light gray)

    ¼ x 1¾ oz (50 g) ball – approx. 50 yd (45 m) – each of shades 18 Teal (blue-green), 30 Pink, 04 Gray

    ⅛ x 1¾ oz (50 g) ball – approx. 25 yd (22.5 m) – each of shades 28 Tangerine, 22 Fuchsia (bright pink), 02 Ecru (off-white), 09 Red (bright red), 32 Leaf (green)

- US size 4 (3.5 mm) circular knitting needle, length 15 in. (37.5 cm)
- Stitch marker
- Yarn sewing needle

gauge (tension)

28 sts and 38 rows over 4 in. (10 cm) square working st st using US size 4 (3.5 mm) needles.

finished size

12¾ x 9 in. (32 x 22.5 cm)

special technique

Jogless stripe

A "jog" is created when knitting from one round to the next and the ends of each round do not stay lined up. On stripe/solid sections, work jogless stripe technique as follows:

Join in new color in first st at beg of round and place st marker. Complete knitting in the round to end as instructed.

Commence new round by picking up first st of previous round (old color), slip same st onto LH needle, and knit both slipped st and first st of next round together.

Chart 1

Key to colors

- ▨ Silver (light gray)
- ■ Teal (blue-green)
- ▨ Pink
- ▨ Gray
- ▨ Tangerine
- ■ Fuchsia (bright pink)
- □ Ecru (off-white)
- ■ Red (bright red)
- ▨ Leaf (green)

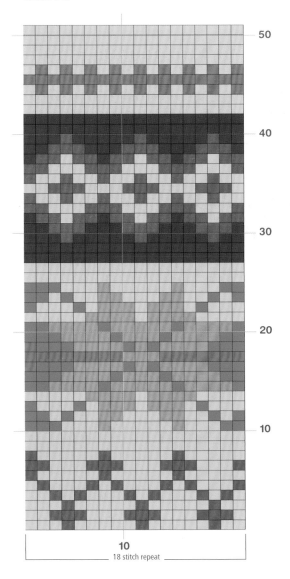

— 20

— 10

4 stitch repeat

Chart 2

— 50

— 40

— 30

— 20

— 10

10
18 stitch repeat

Notes

Chart is read right to left on every row.
Strand colors not in use loosely on WS of work.

Cowl

Using US size 4 (3.5 mm) circular needle, cast on 180 sts and join for working in the round. Place st marker to mark beg of round.

Rounds 1–4: [K1, p1] rib to end.

Using st st, work repeats of rows of Chart 1 and then repeats of rows of Chart 2. Read Chart from right to left and rep each Chart row around the work as instructed. When you reach marker, slip marker st and commence next row as illustrated on Chart.

On Rounds 12, 20, 51, and 66, use jogless stripe technique (see special technique on page 51) to prevent "jumps" in patt.

Next 4 rounds: [K1, p1] rib.

Bind (cast) off.

Finishing

Sew in ends and use them to close any gaps in long sections.

aran cable hat

A very neat little cable hat with bobbles and an edging. I've chosen to work it in two colors, but it works equally well in one color and suits either a man or woman.

materials

- Debbie Bliss Cashmerino Aran (55% merino wool/33% microfiber/12% cashmere) worsted (Aran) yarn
  2:**2** x 1¾ oz (50 g) balls – approx. 98.5 yd (90 m) per ball – of shade 101 Ecru (off-white) (MC)
  1:**1** x 1¾ oz (50 g) ball – approx. 98.5 yd (90 m) – of shade 053 Rose (pink) (CC)
- US size 6 (4 mm) circular needle, length 24 in. (60 cm)
- Cable needle
- Yarn sewing needle

gauge (tension)

18 sts x 30 rows over 4 in. (10 cm) square working st st using US size 6 (4 mm) needles.

finished size

To fit: 1 (woman):**2 (man)**
Head circumference: 19¾ in. (50 cm)
22 in. (56 cm)

special techniques

Cable

C6B – place next 3 sts on CN and hold at back of work, k3, k3 from CN.
C6F – place next 3 sts on CN and hold at front of work, k3, k3 from CN.
C5B – place next 2 sts on CN and hold at back of work, k3, k2 from CN.
C5F – place next 3 sts on CN and hold at front of work, k2, k3 from CN.
C4B – place next 2 sts on CN and hold at back of work, k2, k2 from CN.
C4F – place next 2 sts on CN and hold at front of work, k2, k2 from CN.
C3B – place next 1 st on CN and hold at back of work, k2, k1 from CN.
C3F – place next 2 sts on CN and hold at front of work, k1, k2 from CN.
C2B – place next 1 st on CN and hold at back of work, k1, k1 from CN.
C2F – place next 1 st on CN and hold at front of work, k1, k1 from CN.

Hat

Using CC yarn and US size 6 (4 mm) circular needle, cast on 96:**112** sts. Join in the round, being careful not to twist sts, and mark start of round with scrap yarn or st marker.

Round 1: *K1, p1 (rib); rep from * to end.

Next round: Change to MC and cont in k1, p1 rib for 2 in. (5 cm).

Round 1 of cable patt: [P4, k12] to end.

Rounds 2–4: As Round 1.

Round 5: [P4, C6B, C6F] to end.

Round 6: As Round 1.

Rep Rounds 1–6 another 4:**6** times, then Rounds 1–5 once more.

Decrease section:

Round 1 (dec): [P1, p2tog, p1, k12] to end. (90:**105** sts)

Rounds 2–4: [P3, k12] to end.

Round 5 (dec): [P3, k2tog, k8, ssk] to end. (78:**91** sts)

Round 6: [P3, C5B, C5F] to end.

Round 7: [P3, k10] to end.

Round 8 (dec): [P2tog, p1, k10] to end. (72:**84** sts)

Round 9: [P2, k10] to end.

Round 10 (dec): [P2, k2tog, k6, ssk] to end. (60:**70** sts)

Round 11: [P2, C4B, C4F] to end.

Round 12 (dec): [P2tog, k8] to end. (54:**63** sts)

Round 13: [P1, k8] to end.

Round 14 (dec): [P1, k2tog, k4, ssk] to end. (42:**49** sts)

Round 15: [P1, C3B, C3F] to end.

Round 16: [P1, k6] to end.

Round 17: [K2tog, k5] to end. (36:**42** sts)

Round 18: K to end.

Round 19 (dec): [K2tog, k2, ssk] to end. (24:**28** sts)

Round 20: [C2B, C2F] to end.

Round 21 (dec): [K2tog, ssk] to end. (12:**14** sts)

Round 22 (dec): [K2tog] to end. (6:**7** sts)

Break yarn and thread through rem sts.

Pull closed and fasten off.

Finishing

Weave in ends.

Using CC make 3 small pompoms (see page 62), leaving a long tail end.

Using a yarn sewing needle, thread another long tail of yarn through the bottom of the first pompom so that you have three strands. Braid (plait) the strands for approx. 2 in. (5 cm), knot the end, and thread the strands through the top of the hat to the WS. Secure the ends on the WS of the hat. Rep for the other two pompoms.

toasty-warm gloves

I love Fair Isle gloves. Here I've used Rooster Yarns, a blend of merino and alpaca wool—they are super soft on your skin and the colors look great.

materials

- Rooster Almerino DK (50% baby alpaca/50% merino wool) light worsted (DK) yarn
  - 2 x 1¾ oz (50 g) balls – approx. 124 yd (112.5 m) per ball – of shade 214 Damson (purple) (A)
  - 1 x 1¾ oz (50 g) ball – approx. 124 yd (112.5 m) – each of shades 201 Cornish (off-white) (B), 211 Brighton Rock (pink) (C), 207 Gooseberry (green) (D), 210 Custard (yellow) (E)
- US size 2/3 (3 mm) and US size 5 (3.75 mm) double-pointed needles
- Stitch holder
- Yarn sewing needle

gauge (tension)

25 sts and 26 rows over 4 in. (10 cm) square working Fair Isle patt in st st using US size 5 (3.75 mm) needles.

finished size

To fit size: 1 (woman):**2 (man)**

Notes

Chart is read right to left on every row.
Strand colors not in use loosely on WS of work.
Leave sts on holders and complete thumb and fingers individually.

Left Glove

Using US size 2/3 (3 mm) needles and A, cast on 16:**20** sts on each of first two needles and 20:**24** sts on third needle. (52:**64** sts)
To join in a round, bring yarn to front, sl first st onto third needle, take yarn back between sts, sl first st back onto first needle and turn.
Round 1: [K2, p2] rib to end.
Rib 20:**24** more rounds.
K 1:**2** rounds.
Using B, k 2:**3** rounds.
Change to US size 5 (3.75 mm) needles.
Using A, k 2:**3** rounds.**

Work in patt from Chart 1 (stitches for woman's glove are outlined on Chart 1) as follows:
Round 1: Using A, M1, patt 25:**29** sts of row 1 of Chart 1, using A, M1 and mark this st for thumb gusset (row 1 of Chart 3), patt 27:**35** sts of row 1 of Chart 2. (54:**66** sts)
This round sets position of Charts for palm, thumb, and back patt. Cont in patt from Charts, starting at right-hand edge of Charts on every round and working M1 at each side of thumb gusset as indicated until 15:**17** rounds have been completed. (62:**76** sts)
Next round: Using A, k1, patt 25:**29** sts of Chart 1, sl next 9:**11** sts of thumb gusset onto st holder, using A cast on 4:**6** sts, patt 27:**35** sts of Chart 2. (57:**71** sts)
***Cont in patt, knit cast-on sts above thumb in A on every round, until final rounds of Charts 1 and 2 have been completed.
K 2:**3** rounds using A.
Change to US size 2/3 (3 mm) needles.
Using B, k 2:**3** rounds.
Cont in A, k 4:**6** rounds.
Divide for fingers:
Little finger: With first needle – k7:**8**, with second needle – cast on 3 sts, leave next 44:**56** sts of round on st holder, with second needle – k next st, with third needle – k last 5:**7** sts. (16:**18** sts)
K 20:**24** rounds.

Dec round: [Sl 2, k1, p2sso] 5:**6** times, k1:**0**. (6:**6** sts)
Cut yarn, leaving a long tail. Thread end through sts, draw up,
and secure.

Ring finger: With first needle – k first 7:**9** sts from st holder, leave
next 30:**38** sts on holder and sl last 7:**9** sts onto a spare needle,
with second needle – cast on 3 sts, k4 from spare needle, with third
needle – k3:**5** from spare needle, k up 4 sts from base of 3 sts cast
on for previous finger. (21:**25** sts)
Knit 1 round.
Round 2: K7:**9**, sl 2, k1, p2sso, k8:**10**, sl 2, k1, p2sso. (17:**21** sts)
K 24:**28** rounds.
Dec round: [K2tog] 1:**0** times, [sl 2, k1, p2sso] 5:**7** times. (6:**7** sts)
Fasten off as Little Finger.

Middle finger: With first needle – leaving center 16:**20** sts on
holder, work as given for Ring Finger but completing 26:**30** rounds
before working dec round.

Forefinger: With first needle – k6:**8** from holder, with second
needle – k next 6:**8** sts from holder, with third needle – k last 4 sts
from holder, k up 3 sts from cast-on sts of Middle Finger. (19:**23** sts)
K 1 round.
Round 2: K16:**20**, sl 2, k1, p2sso. (17:**21** sts)
Complete as Ring Finger.

Thumb: With first needle – k9:**11** from st holder, with second
needle – k up 3 sts from row ends and 2:**3** sts from first 2:**3** cast-on
sts, with third needle – k up 2:**3** sts from next 2:**3** cast-on sts and
3 sts from row ends. (19:**23** sts)
K 18:**22** rounds.
Dec round: [Sl2, k1, p2sso] 6:**7** times, k1:**0**, [k2tog] 0:**1** times.
(7:**8** sts)
Fasten off as Little Finger.

Right Glove
Work as given for Left Glove to **.
Work in patt from Chart as foll:
Round 1: Patt 27:**35** sts as row 1 of Chart 2, using A, M1 and
mark this st for thumb gusset (row 1 of Chart 3), patt 25:**29** sts of
row 1 of Chart 1, using A, M1. (54:**66** sts)
This round sets position of Charts for back, thumb, and palm patt.
Cont in patt from Charts, working M1 at each side of thumb gusset
as indicated, until 15:**17** rounds have been completed. (62:**76** sts)
Next round: Patt 27:**3**5 sts of Chart 2, sl next 9:**11** sts of thumb
gusset onto a st holder, with A cast on 4:**6** sts, patt 25:**29** sts of
Chart 1, k1 in A. (57:**71** sts)
Complete as given for Left Glove from *** to end.

Finishing
Press and sew in any ends.

Chart 2 women's glove

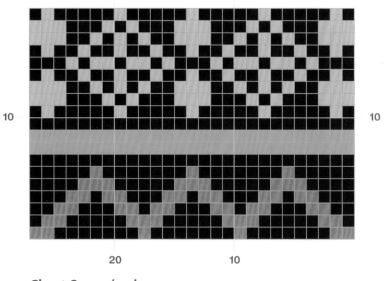

10   10

20   10

Key to colors

■ Damson (purple)

□ Cornish (off-white)

■ Brighton Rock (pink)

■ Gooseberry (green)

■ Custard (yellow)

Chart 2 men's glove

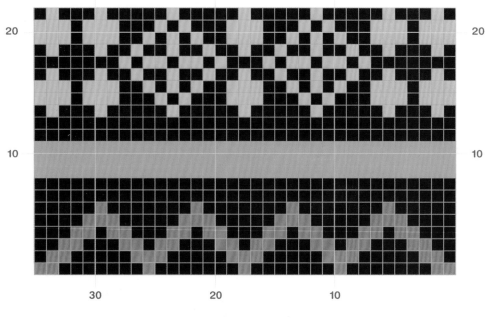

20   20

10   10

30   20   10

Chart 3 women's glove

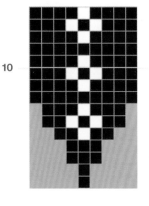

10   10

Chart 3 men's glove

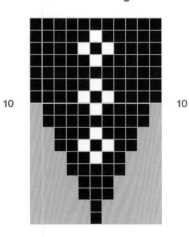

10   10

10

Key to colors

■ no stitch

□ Cornish (off-white)

■ Damson (purple)

Chart 1

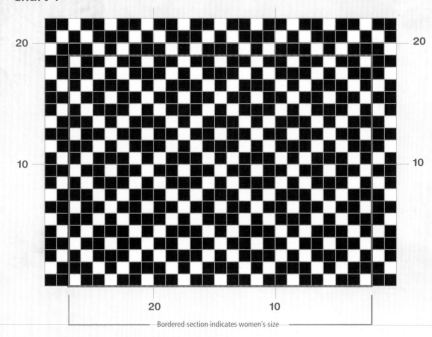

Key to colors

☐ Cornish (off-white)

■ Damson (purple)

Bordered section indicates women's size

back of hand

palm of hand

light as a feather scarf

Mohair isn't the easiest yarn to work Fair Isle in, but I couldn't resist just a little design. It's best to practice first using plain yarn, because mohair is really difficult to undo. This scarf is worked on a circular needle, which creates a tube, so it's light and flexible but also lovely and thick.

materials

- Debbie Bliss Angel (76% super kid mohair/24% silk lace) laceweight yarn

  3 x ⅞ oz (25 g) balls – approx. 219 yd (200 m) per ball – of shade 05 Stone (off-white) (MC)

  1 x ⅞ oz (25 g) ball – approx. 219 yd (200 m) – each of shades 09 Aqua (blue), 13 Coral (light pink), 20 Scarlet (red), 27 Teal (green-blue), 12 Lime (green), 36 Heather (purple)
- US size 5 (3.75 mm) circular needle, length 16 in. (40 cm)
- Yarn sewing needle

gauge (tension)

26 sts x 31 rows over 4 in. (10 cm) square working Fair Isle patt in st st using US size 5 (3.75 mm) needle.

finished size

Approx. 56¾ x 6¾ in. (143 x 17 cm)

Scarf

Using MC, cast on 84 sts and join for circular knitting, placing a st marker at the beg of first round and taking care not to twist work. Work in st st for 20 rounds.
Work from Chart, foll patt rep along round and color combinations as directed.
Using MC, work in st st until work measures approx. 45¾ in. (116 cm) from cast-on edge.
Turn Chart upside down and follow patt for other end (mirroring design of first end).
Using MC work in st st for 20 rounds.
Bind (cast) off.

Finishing
Sew in ends.

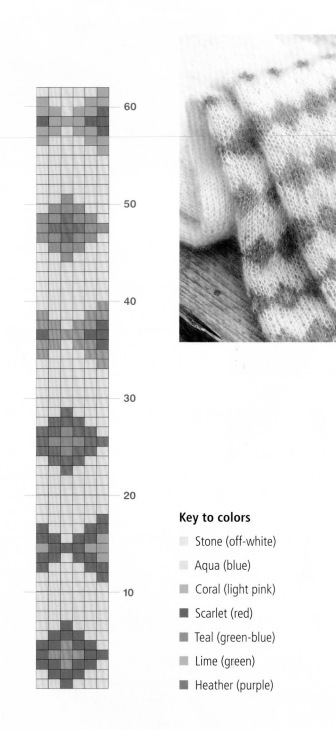

Key to colors

- Stone (off-white)
- Aqua (blue)
- Coral (light pink)
- Scarlet (red)
- Teal (green-blue)
- Lime (green)
- Heather (purple)

swiss check scarf

This is a great way to begin using color. There's no need to "carry" your yarn across each row—the pattern on this scarf uses a slip stitch technique so you're only working with one strand at a time.

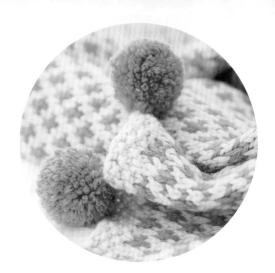

materials

- Rooster Almerino Aran (50% baby alpaca/50% merino wool) worsted (Aran) yarn
  - 2 x 1¾ oz (50 g) balls – approx. 103 yd (94 m) per ball – of shade 315 Shimmer (light gray) (A)
  - 2 x 1¾ oz (50 g) balls – approx.103 yd (94 m) per ball – of shade 318 Coral (orange) (B)
  - 1 x 1¾ oz (50 g) ball – approx. 98.5 yd (90 m) – of shade 316 Lagoon (turquoise) (C)
- US size 8 (5 mm) knitting needles
- Yarn sewing needle

gauge (tension)

22 sts and 24 rows over 4 in. (10 cm) square working Swiss Check stitch using US size 8 (5 mm) needles.

finished size

60¾ x 6¾ in. (154 x 17 cm)

Notes
Make sure you keep the yarn behind the slip stitches loose across the back on Rows 2 and 6.

Scarf
Using A, cast on 37 sts.
Work 4 rows of seed (moss) stitch as follows: [k1, p1] to last st, k1.
Row 1: Using A, purl to end.
Row 2: Using B, k1, sl 1 purlwise, *k1, sl 3 purlwise; rep from * to last 3 sts, k1, sl 1 purlwise, k1.
Row 3: Using B, k1, *p3, sl 1 purlwise; rep from * to last 4 sts, p3, k1.
Row 4: Using A, k2, * sl 1 purlwise, k3: rep from * to last 3 sts, sl 1 purlwise, k2.
Row 5: Using A, purl to end.
Row 6: Using B, k1, *sl 3 purlwise, k1: rep from * to end.
Row 7: Using B, k1, pl, *sl 1 purlwise, p3; rep from * to last 3 sts, sl 1 purlwise, p1, k1.
Row 8: Using A, k4, *sl 1 purlwise, k3; rep from * to last st, k1.
Rep Rows 1–8 until work measures approx. 60 in. (150 cm).
Cont with A, work 4 rows of seed (moss) stitch.
Bind (cast) off.

Pompoms
(make 6)
Drape a length of C over three fingers with palm facing up, with a long tail (approx 6 in./15 cm) at the front. Wrap yarn round fingers approx 65 times. Slide loops off fingers carefully, holding them in one hand. Wrap a length of C around the center tightly approx 8 times. Cut yarn, leaving a tail approx. 12 in. (30 cm). Thread yarn tail into yarn sewing needle and push needle through center wrap 4 or 5 times to secure. Tie both tails tightly in a double knot. Unthread needle from yarn. Holding tails, cut through loops on both sides. Continue to hold tails and trim ends carefully to a pompom shape to make a pompom approx 2 in. (5 cm) in diameter.

Finishing
Attach three pompoms to each end of the scarf – one at each end and one in the middle. Sew the pompoms loosely to scarf ends so they are not too tight against the edge of the scarf. Sew in ends.

psychedelic socks

These great socks are colorful and the pattern is easy to follow. They use up only small amounts of each color yarn, so you will have plenty left over to make gifts for your friends and family.

materials

- Artesano Definition Sock Yarn (75% machine washable merino wool/25% polyamide) fingering (4-ply) yarn
  ¼ x 3½ oz (100 g) hank – 109.5 yd (100 m) – each of shades 8362 Mushy Peas (lime green) (A), SFN10 Cream Cake (cream) (B), 0042 Inferno (red) (C), 6705 Azure (turquoise) (D)
  ⅛ x 3½ oz (100 g) hank – 55 yd (50 m) – each of shades 4967 Denim (blue) (E), 4908 Perky (bright pink) (F), 2083 Kimono (dark pink) (G), 6701 Peacock (dark blue) (H)
- US size 1/2 (2.5 mm) circular sock knitting needle, length 16 in. (40 cm)
- 3 x US size 1/2 (2.5 mm) double-pointed needles
- Stitch marker

gauge (tension)

28 sts x 36 rows over 4 in. (10 cm) square working Fair Isle patt in st st using US size 1/2 (2.5 mm) needles.

finished size

To fit women's size: US 7.5–8.5 (UK 5–6)
Foot length: 10¼ in. (25.5 cm)
Heel to top: 12 in. (30 cm)
Width of foot: 9½ in. (24 cm)

special techniques

Wrap
A wrap stitch is used to turn a short row heel. This short row wrap technique is used when you need to turn before you get to the end and the wrap prevents the gap between the stitches.
Follow the patt as instructed to sts before the turn.
For knit rows: with yarn at the back of work, sl next st purlwise from left to right needle, bring yarn to front of work, place slipped st back on left-hand needle, turn.
For purl rows: with yarn at front of work, sl next st purlwise from left to right needle, take yarn to back of work, place slipped st back on left-hand needle, turn.

Notes
This pattern is knitted in rounds, so you will only be knitting on the front (RS) of the work, which makes it easier to follow the Chart. Read the Charts from right to left at beg of each round. This pattern has a fairly large cuff that holds the sock up better. You could also buy very thin knitting elastic, which can be knitted alongside the yarn in the rib.
If you'd like to knit the sock longer, just add more stripes.
When you get to the heel, divide the heel from the in-step and work the heel flat, knitting the front (RS) and purling the back (WS) before rejoining it to the circular needle.
Remember that yarn stretches, so this size sock is also suitable for slightly larger sizes.

Sock
(make 1 pair)
Start at the toe. Using A and US size 1/2 (2.5 mm) needles, cast on 32 sts with long tail cast on method (see page 120). Divide between two double-pointed needles, 16 sts on each.
Round 1: First needle – k1, M1, k to last st, M1, k1, second needle – rep as for first needle.

Round 2: K one round without inc.

Rep Rounds 1–2 until there are 64 sts (32 sts on each needle).

Rounds 16–19: K to end.

Change to US size 2/3 (2.5 mm) circular needle.

Place a marker to mark the beg of each round.

Using E, B, and F, k five rows of Chart 1 to end.

Cont in G.

Next 3 rounds: K to end.

Next round: [K16, M1] 4 times. (68 sts)

Next round: K to end. (68 sts)

Using C, H, and B, k eight rows of Chart 2 to end.

Next 5 Rounds: Using F, k to end.

Using D, A, and E, k eleven rows of Chart 3 to end.

Using H, work Row 1 of Chart 4 as follows: [K17, M1] 4 times. (72 sts)

Using H and G, k rem seven rows of Chart 4 to end.

Using B, A, and F, k five rows of Chart 5 to end.

Next 3 rounds: Using E, k to end.

Next round: Using C, k to end.

Next 2 rounds: Using E, k to end.

Next round: Using C, k to end.

Next 2 rounds: Using E, k to end.

Divide for heel:

Keep first 36 heel sts on working needle (either circular needle or double-pointed needle) and leave 36 in-step sts on a st holder. When working the heel you will not be working in the round. Working st st on 36 heel sts only and using A, work shaping as follows:

Row 1: K35, wrap last st, turn.

Row 2: Sl wrapped st, p34, wrap last st, turn.

Rep last two rows, reducing number of sts on each row until 15 sts rem unwrapped in center; these form first part of heel.

Next row: K across 15 sts to first unworked and wrapped st. Pick up wrap on left needle with its unworked st and knit both together, wrap next st, turn. (This st has been wrapped twice.)

(NB: The wrap is a wrap laying at the base of the st—no wrapped sts are worked sts.)

Next row: Slip first double wrapped st, p across to first unworked wrapped st, pick up wrap, purl tog with its st, turn.

Cont in this way, picking up both wraps and k or p tog with corresponding st. When all 36 sts have been worked, heel is complete.

At end of heel shaping, on first Round when all sts are ready to be worked, pick up 1 extra st at both joins between heel sts and unworked in-step sts and work together with next st to avoid any holes. (72 sts)

Transfer all sts back to circular needle.

Work ankle:

Next 2 rounds: Using E, k to end.

Next 5 rounds: Using C, k to end.

Next 3 rounds: Using A, k to end.

Using C and G, k nine rows of Chart 6 to end.

Using D and F, k seven rows of Chart 7 to end.

Starting at st 5, using D, B, and H, k eleven rows of Chart 8 to end.

Next 3 rounds: Using G, k to end.

Next round: [K18, M1] 4 times. (76 sts)

Next 2 rounds: K to end.

Using B, A, and F, k five rows of Chart 5 to end.

Cont in E.

Next round: K to end.

Next round: [K38, M1] twice. (78 sts)

Using B, E, and D, k eleven rows of Chart 9 to end.

Next round: Using G, k to end.

Next round: Using C, [K39, M1] twice. (80 sts)

Using D, F, and H, k seventeen rows of Chart 10 to end.

Ribbed cuff:

Next 9 rounds: Using A, k1, p1 (rib) to end.

Bind (cast) off loosely.

Finishing

Block and press.

Chart 1

Key to colors

- ◼ Mushy Peas (lime green)
- ☐ Cream Cake (cream)
- ◼ Inferno (red)
- ◼ Azure (turquoise)
- ◼ Denim (blue)
- ◼ Perky (bright pink)
- ◼ Kimono (dark pink)
- ◼ Peacock (dark blue)

Chart 2

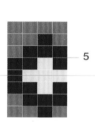

Chart 3

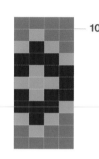

Chart 4

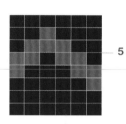

Chart 5

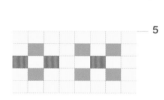

Chart 6

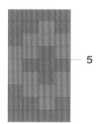

Chart 7

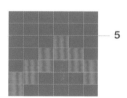

Chart 8

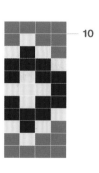

Chart 9

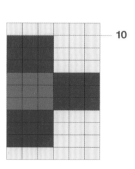

Chart 10

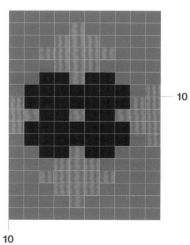

reindeer bag

This is such a fun design—reindeers and hearts seem to go together in many Nordic designs. This is a good size bag featuring a traditional Scandinavian-style pattern.

materials

- Debbie Bliss Rialto Chunky (100% extra-fine merino wool) bulky (chunky) yarn
    - 4 x 1¾ oz (50 g) balls – approx. 66 yd (60 m) per ball – of shade 003 Ecru (white) (MC)
    - 2 x 1¾ oz (50 g) balls – approx. 66 yd (60 m) per ball – of shade 022 Storm (gray) (A)
    - 1 x 1¾ oz (50 g) ball – approx. 66 yd (60 m) – each of shades 007 Gold (yellow), 018 Teal (blue-green), 015 Ruby (red)
- US size 9 (5.5 mm) and US size 10 (6 mm) knitting needles
- Moda Domestic Bliss 100% cotton fabric, 20 in. (50 cm) of Floral Kitchenette Blue code 18072-17
- Yarn sewing needle
- Sewing needle
- Matching sewing thread

gauge (tension)

18 sts x 24 rows over 4 in. (10 cm) square working st st using US size 10 (6 mm) needles.

finished size

14¼ x 11 in. (36 x 28 cm)

Notes

Chart is read right to left on odd-numbered (RS) rows and left to right on even-numbered (WS) rows.

Strand colors not in use loosely on WS of work.

Knit tightly in one-color sections to balance out the gauge (tension) difference with the stranded colorwork sections, which should be knitted loosely.

Knit the Reindeer using the intarsia technique (see page 123) rather than Fair Isle to avoid the "bleed" of gray into the white background.

Front and Back

(make 2 the same)

Using US size 10 (6 mm) needles and A, cast on 65 sts.

Working in st st throughout, follow the Chart.

Next 5 rows: Using MC, work seed (moss) stitch as follows: [k1, p1] to last st, k1.

Bind (cast) off.

Handles

(make 2 the same)

Using US size 9 (5.5 mm) needles and MC, cast on 7 sts.

Work in seed (moss) st for 114 rows or until work measures 17 in. (43.5 cm).

Bind (cast) off.

Finishing

Measure Front knitted piece. From the lining fabric, cut two pieces the same size as Front knitted piece plus ⅝ in. (1.5cm) extra on each edge for seam allowances.

Measure Handle knitted piece. From the lining fabric cut two pieces the same size as Handle knitted piece, plus double the width and with extra ⅜ in. (1 cm) at each end.

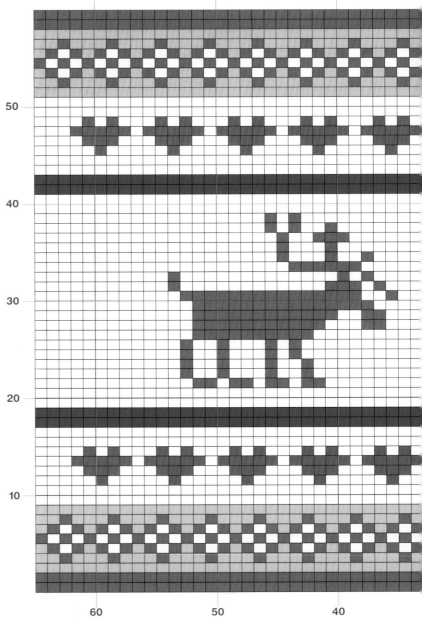

Lining:
With RS together, pin and sew Front and Back lining along two sides and bottom, leaving top open, taking a ⅝-in. (1.5-cm) seam allowance throughout. Cut across bottom corners diagonally, being careful not to cut through stitching. Press seams open.
Fold ⅝ in. (1.5 cm) over to WS along top edge and press.
Fold both long sides of one piece of Handle lining over to meet at the center, with WS together, and press. Pin lining to knitted Handle, with raw edges of lining facing the knitting. Repeat for the other Handle and then sew lining onto each Handle using whipstitch.

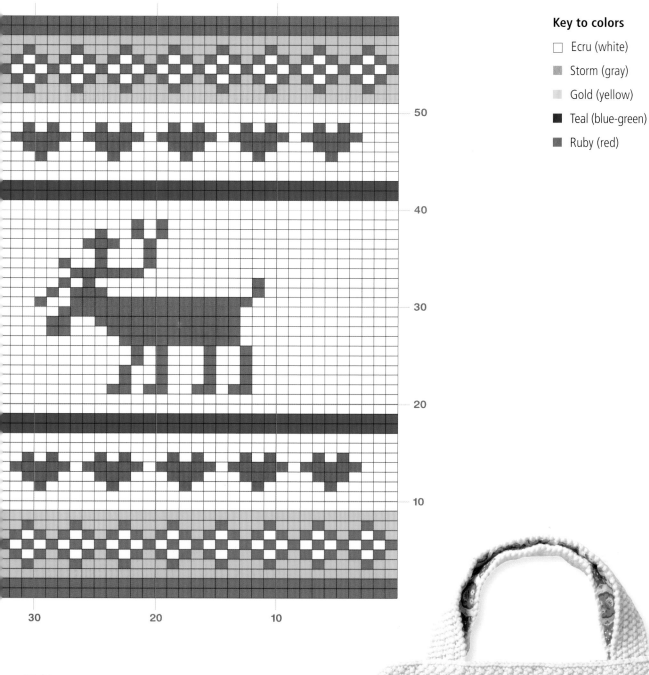

Key to colors

☐ Ecru (white)

▨ Storm (gray)

▧ Gold (yellow)

■ Teal (blue-green)

▦ Ruby (red)

Making up:

Sew the Front and Back of the knitted bag together using mattress stitch. Fit fabric lining inside knitted bag with WS together and pin around top edge.

Insert about 1 in. (2.5 cm) of each end of first Handle between Front and Front lining about 2½ in. (6.5 cm) from side seams, and pin in place. Repeat for second Handle on Back. Hand sew lining to top of bag, securing Handles in place by stitching twice across the top of each end.

CHAPTER 3
for the home

heirloom blanket

This beautiful blanket is the perfect size to wrap your baby in, or to drape in a buggy or car seat to keep your little one cozy and warm. You'll want to keep it forever.

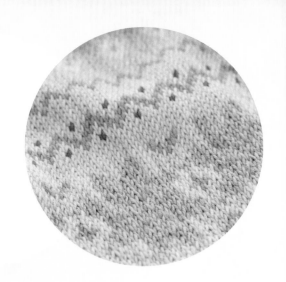

materials

- Debbie Bliss Baby Cashmerino (55% merino wool/33% microfiber/12% cashmere) light worsted (DK) yarn
    7 x 1¾ oz (50 g) balls – approx. 137 yd (125 m) per ball – of shade 012 Silver (pale gray) (MC)
    2 x 1¾ oz (50 g) balls – approx. 137 yd (125 m) per ball – of shade 204 Baby Blue (pale blue)
    1 x 1¾ oz (50 g) ball – approx. 137 yd (125 m) – each of shades 078 Lipstick (deep pink), 001 Primrose (yellow), 068 Peach Melba (peach), 002 Apple (green), 006 Candy Pink (bright pink), 059 Mallard (dark blue), 034 Bright Red, 101 Ecru (off-white)
- US size 3 (3.25 mm) knitting needles
- Yarn sewing needle

gauge (tension)

25 sts x 27 rows over 4 in. (10 cm) square working Fair Isle patt in st st using US size 3 (3.25 mm) needles.

finished size

38½ x 35½ in. (97.5 x 90 cm)

Notes
Chart is read right to left on odd-numbered (RS) rows and left to right on even-numbered (WS) rows. Follow Charts 1–12. Strand colors not in use loosely on WS of work.

Blanket
Using MC, cast on 244 sts.
Work in seed (moss) st for 14 rows.
Cont to work seed (moss) st for 10 sts each side of 224 sts of chart, working chart in st st between, creating seed (moss) st border.
Cont patt on charts 1–12 until work measures approx. 34 in. (86 cm).
Work in seed (moss) st for 14 rows.
Bind (cast) off.

Finishing
Sew in ends.

top tip
Use a row counter on the end of your needle to keep track of where you are in the pattern. If you don't have a row counter, you can strike off the numbers down the right side of the chart as you complete the rows.

Chart 1

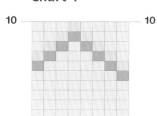

Chart 2

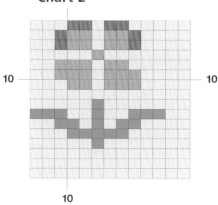

Chart 3

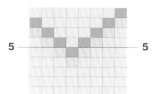

Charts 4 and 6

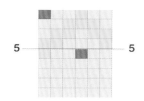

Chart 5

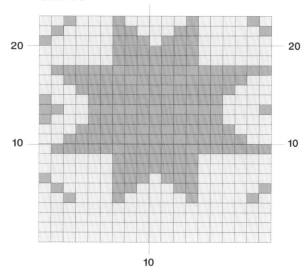

Key to colors

- Silver (pale gray)
- Baby Blue (pale blue)
- Lipstick (deep pink)
- Primrose (yellow)
- Peach Melba (peach)
- Apple (green)
- Candy Pink (bright pink)
- Mallard (dark blue)
- Bright Red
- Ecru (off-white)

Chart 7

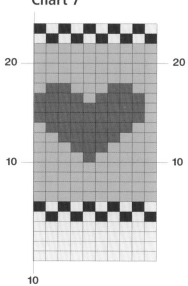

Chart 8

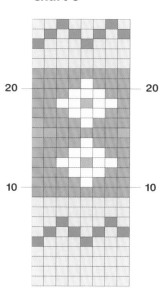

Chart 9

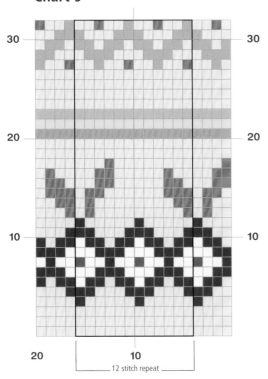

12 stitch repeat

Chart 10

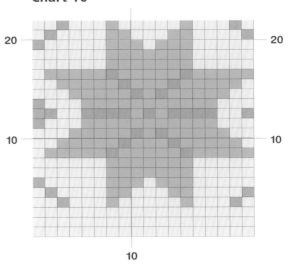

Chart 11

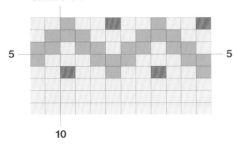

Chart 12

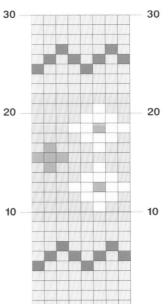

Key to colors

- Silver (pale gray)
- Baby Blue (pale blue)
- Lipstick (deep pink)
- Primrose (yellow)
- Peach Melba (peach)
- Apple (green)
- Candy Pink (bright pink)
- Mallard (dark blue)
- Bright Red
- Ecru (off-white)

kindle cover

A knitted cover is a great way to protect your Kindle or other e-reader device—and this makes a great gift, too.

materials

- Rooster Almerino DK (50% baby alpaca/50% merino wool) light worsted (DK) yarn
    1 x 1¾ oz (50 g) ball – approx. 124 yd (112.5 m) – each of shades 218 Starfish (orange) (MC), 201 Cornish (off-white), 217 Beach (turquoise)
- US size 6 (4 mm) knitting needles
- Yarn sewing needle
- 1 fat quarter lining fabric Moda Domestic Bliss 18072-17
- 1 yd (1 m) bobble edging
- 1 yd (1 m) of 1-in. (2.5-cm) wide orange gingham ribbon
- Sewing needle and neutral thread

gauge (tension)

23 sts and 20 rows over 4 in. (10 cm) square working Fair Isle pattern in st st using US size 6 (4 mm) needles.

finished size

5½ x 7½ in. (14 x 19 cm)

Notes

Chart is read right to left on odd-numbered (RS) rows and left to right on even-numbered (WS) rows.

Strand colors not in use loosely on WS of work.

Measure the length and the width of the device. This pattern is based on an e-reader measuring approx. 6¾ x 4¾ x ⅜ in. (17 x 12 x 1 cm), but use the gauge (tension) as a guide to number of stitches needed at cast on. Measure the width of your device and continue until the length matches the length of your device.

If your device is much bigger than the size specified here you will need more yarn.

top tip

If the cover is for a different device, measure the length, width and depth to determine the length and width of the finished cover. Then add 1⅜ in. (3.5 cm) to both these dimensions and cut two pieces of lining fabric to these measurements.

Front and Back

(make 2 the same)

Using MC, cast on 33 sts.

Next row: P to end.

Rows 1–36: Foll Chart.

Next row: Using MC, k to end.

Bind (cast) off.

Finishing

Block and lightly press Front and Back to make them the same size.

Sew in all ends.

Place Front and Back knitted pieces RS together and join side and bottom seams using MC and yarn sewing needle. Turn RS out.

Lining:

Cut the lining fabric into two pieces, each 8¼ x 6½ in. (21 x 16.5 cm). Place lining pieces RS together and pin along sides and bottom edges. Sew sides and bottom, taking a ⅝-in. (1.5-cm) seam allowance. Press seams open. Fold ⅝ in. (1.5 cm) to WS along top edge and press.

Making up:

Place fabric lining inside knitted piece with WS together.

Pin bobble edging along top edge between lining fabric and knitted piece, so top of bobble edging is showing around top edge.

Cut ribbon in half and place one end of one length in center of top edge between lining and knitted piece. Place other length to correspond with first on other side.

Pin and hand sew top edge of lining to top edge of knitted piece, using a sewing needle and neutral thread and incorporating bobble edging and ribbon.

Key to colors

- ■ Starfish (orange)
- □ Cornish (off-white)
- ■ Beach (turquoise)

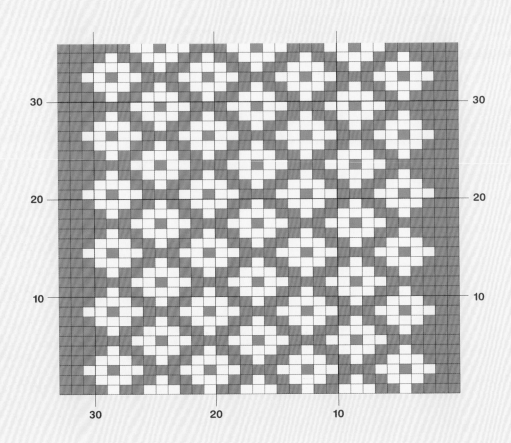

nordic bunting

These little flags are great for beginners wishing to practice Fair Isle, because they knit up very quickly and the Fair Isle designs are very simple to follow.

materials

- Debbie Bliss Rialto DK (100% extra-fine merino wool) light worsted (DK) yarn
  ⅓ x 1¾ oz (50 g) ball – approx. 38.5 yd (35 m) – each of shades 50 Deep Rose (bright pink), 12 Scarlet (red), 45 Gold (yellow), 58 Grass (green)
  ¼ x 1¾ oz (50 g) ball – approx. 29 yd (26.5 m) – of shade 44 Aqua (mid blue)
  ⅛ x 1¾ oz (50 g) ball – approx. 14.5 yd (13 m) – each of shades 51 Indigo (dark blue), 43 Burnt Orange (orange), 02 Ecru (off-white), 66 Vintage Pink (pale pink)
- US size 6 (4 mm) knitting needles
- 20 in. (50 cm) yellow cotton gingham lining fabric
- 2¾ yd (2.5 m) of ⅞-in. (25-mm) wide yellow bias binding

gauge (tension)

25 sts and 27 rows over 4 in. (10 cm) square working st st using US size 6 (4 mm) needles.

finished size

Each flag measures approx. 5 in. (13 cm) across top edge and 6¾ in. (17 cm) down each side

Notes

Chart is read right to left on odd-numbered (RS) rows and left to right on even-numbered (WS) rows.
Strand colors not in use loosely on WS of work.

Flags

(make 1 in each design)
Cast on 33 sts and work in st st throughout.
Follow 46 rows of each Chart for placement of Fair Isle patt.
Row 1 (RS): K to end.
Row 2: K1, p to last st, k1.
Row 3: K1, skpo, k to last 3 sts, k2tog, k1.
Row 4: As Row 2.
Row 5: As Row 1.
Row 6: K1, p2tog, p to last 3 sts, p2tog tbl, k1.
Rep these 6 rows until 5 sts rem.
Work 2 rows straight.
Next row: K1, skpo, k2tog. (3 sts)
K3 tog and fasten off.

Finishing

Block, press, and starch each flag.
Lining:
Place each flag on top of fabric and draw a pencil line approx. ¼ in. (5 mm) larger all around shape of bunting. Cut out fabric.
With WS of fabric facing, press bottom tip upward approx. ¼ in. (5 mm). Fold and press each raw edge inward, creating a tip at the bottom and pressing each of the top edges neatly to create the triangle shape.
Place WS of lining on WS of knitted bunting flag. Pin and hand sew lining to flag using whip stitch or slipstitch.
Rep for all bunting flags.
Making up:
With WS tog, fold binding in half lengthwise and press. Open out binding, pin and sew flags with top edge lined up along fold line, with flags evenly spaced along length, leaving a length at each end for the ties.

Key to colors

- ■ Deep Rose (bright pink)
- ■ Scarlet (red)
- ■ Gold (yellow)
- ■ Grass (green)
- ■ Aqua (mid blue)
- ■ Indigo (dark blue)
- ■ Burnt Orange (orange)
- □ Ecru (off-white)
- ■ Vintage Pink (pale pink)

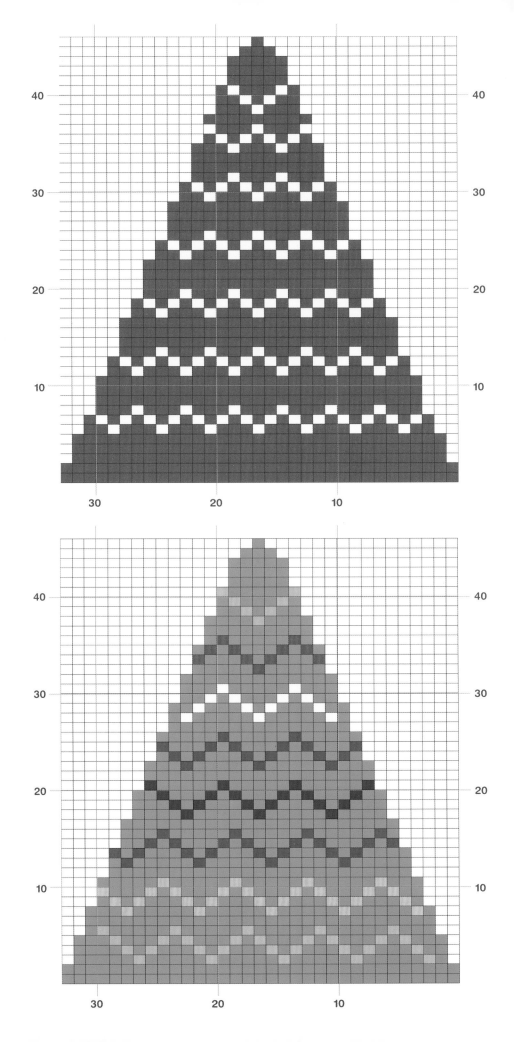

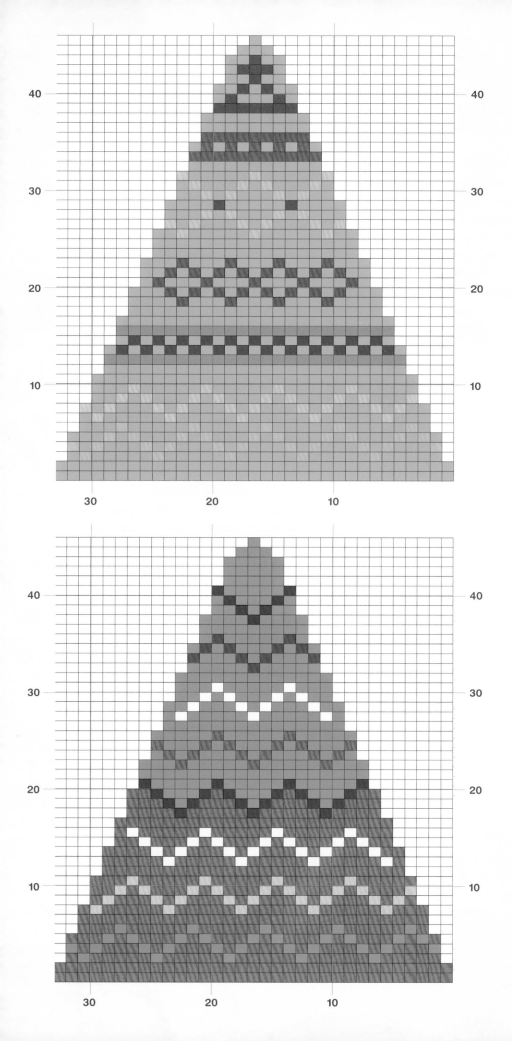

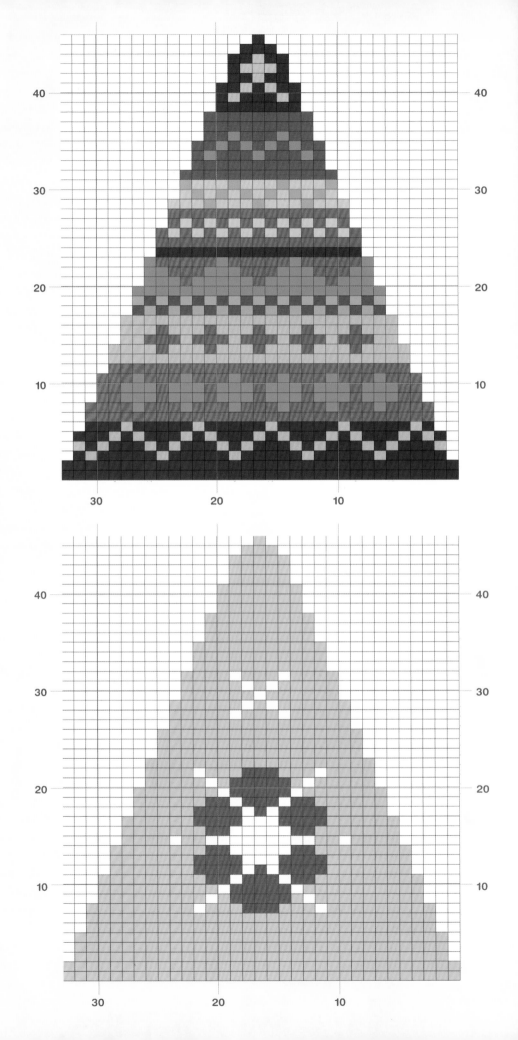

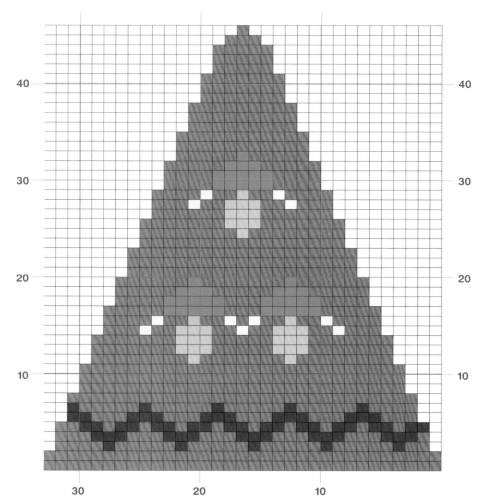

Key to colors

- ■ Deep Rose (bright pink)
- ■ Scarlet (red)
- ■ Gold (yellow)
- ■ Grass (green)
- ■ Aqua (mid blue)
- ■ Indigo (dark blue)
- ■ Burnt Orange (orange)
- □ Ecru (off-white)
- ■ Vintage Pink (pale pink)

little miss mouse

A bag, a hat, a Fair Isle jacket—what more does a mouse need? Try making lots of these, using different colors on the jacket. She makes a wonderful gift.

materials

- Debbie Bliss Donegal Luxury Tweed Aran (90% wool/10% angora) worsted (Aran) yarn
    1 x 1¾ oz (50 g) ball – approx. 96.5 yd (88 m) – of shade 42 Pebble (dark gray) (MC)
- Debbie Bliss Rialto DK (100% extra-fine merino wool) light worsted (DK) yarn
    1 x 1¾ oz (50 g) ball – approx. 115 yd (105 m) – each of shades 20 Teal (dark blue) (A), 50 Deep Rose (bright pink) (C), 45 Gold (yellow) (D)
    Small amounts of each of shades 20 Teal (dark blue) (E), 55 Coral (pale orange), 45 Gold (yellow), 19 Duck Egg (light blue), 53 Basil (green)
- Debbie Bliss Blue Faced Leicester Aran (100% superwash wool) worsted (Aran) yarn
    1 x 1¾ oz (50 g) ball – approx. 82 yd (75 m) – of shade 01 Ecru (off-white) (B)
- US size 5 (3.75 mm) and US size 3 (3.25 mm) knitting needles
- Yarn sewing needle
- Small amount of black and pink yarn
- 3 small buttons

gauge (tension)

25 sts and 27 rows over 4 in. (10 cm) square using st st on US size 3 (3.25 mm) needles.

Notes
Chart is read right to left on odd-numbered (RS) rows and left to right on even-numbered (WS) rows.
Strand colors not in use loosely on WS of work.

Body
Starting at neck edge, using MC and US size 3 (3.25 mm) needles, cast on 16 sts.
Starting with a k row, work two rows st st.
Next row: Inc in every 4th st. (20 sts)
Work 3 rows st st.
Next row: Inc into first st, *K2, inc 1 in next st; rep from * to last st, k1. (27 sts)
Work 3 rows straight st st.
Next row: Inc into each st. (54 sts)
Work 2 rows st st.
With WS facing, k 1 row for waistline.
Work straight from waistline for 1⅜ in. (3.5 cm).
Foll Chart 1 rep for skirt border, ending RS rows and beg WS rows at st 2.
Work 2 more rows st st.
With WS facing, k 1 row for edge of base (this creates a seam line).
Base shaping:
Row 1: *K4, k2tog; rep from * to end. (45 sts)
Row 2 and each foll even row: P to end.
Row 3: *K3, k2tog; rep from * to end. (36 sts)
Row 5: *K2, k2tog; rep from * to end. (27 sts)
Row 7: *K1, k2tog; rep from * to end. (18 sts)
Row 9: K2tog to end. (9 sts)
Leaving long end for sewing up Body, break off yarn and thread through rem 9 sts on needle.

Head
Starting at back of Head, using B and US size 3 (3.25 mm) needles, cast on 12 sts.
Beg with a p row, work 3 rows st st.
Next row: Inc in every st. (24 sts)
Work 3 rows straight in st st.
Next row: Inc in every st. (48 sts)
Work 7 rows straight in st st.

Next row: *K1, k2tog, k1; rep from * to end. (36 sts)
Work 3 rows straight in st st.
Next row: *K2, k2tog; rep from * to end (27 sts)
Work 3 rows straight in st st.
Next row: *K2, k2tog; rep from * to last 3 sts, k2tog, k1. (20 sts)
Work 2 rows straight in st st.
Next row: P2tog to end. (10 sts)
Leave a long end for sewing up head, thread through rem sts and draw up for snout.

Feet
(make 2 the same)
Using B and US size 3 (3.25 mm) needles, cast on 4 sts.
K 1 row.
Work in st st, inc 1 st at each end of foll 2 rows. (8 sts)
Work 10 rows straight in st st.
Dec 1 st at each end of foll 2 rows. (4 sts)
Work one row.
Break yarn and thread through rem 4 sts.

Cardigan
Using E and US size 5 (3.75 mm) needles, cast on 55 sts.
Next row: K (this forms garter st hem of cardigan so it won't curl).
Next 15 rows: Beg with a k row, foll rows of Chart 2, ending RS rows and beg WS rows at st 7.
Work 3 rows st st using E and starting with a p row.
Next row: K1, k2tog, *k3, k2tog; rep from * until 2 sts rem, k2. (44 sts)
Work 3 rows straight in st st.
Next row: K2tog to end. (22 sts)
Next row: P.
Next row: Bind (cast) off 5 sts, *k2tog. (2 sts on needle)
Lift back st over front st, as you do when binding (casting) off. You should have one "live" st left on the needle; rep from * to last 5 sts (including "live" st").
Bind (cast) off rem 5 sts.

Arms
(make 2)
Using E and US size 5 (3.75 mm) needles, cast on 3 sts.
Work 2 rows in st st.
Inc 1 st at each end of the next 6 rows. (15 sts)
Work 8 rows straight in st st.
Next row: *K1, k2tog; rep from * to end. (10 sts).
Next row (WS facing): K rem 10 sts to make garter st sleeve edge.
Break off E, join B.
Work 6 rows in st st.
Break off yarn, thread through rem stitches and pull up tightly.

Ears
(Make 2)
Using B and US size 5 (3.75 mm) needles, cast on 14 sts.
Work 2 rows in st st.
Dec row: K1, [sl 1, k2tog, psso] 4 times, k1. (6 sts)
Bind (cast) off.

Scarf
Using C and US size 5 (3.75 mm) needles, cast on 50 sts.
K1 row.
Bind (cast) off.

Handbag
(make 2)
Using D and US size 5 (3.75 mm) needles, cast on 10 sts.
Work in seed (moss) st as foll:
Row 1: [K1, p1] to end.
Row 2: [P1, k1] to end.
Rep these two rows 5 times more.
Bind (cast) off.

Handle
(make 1)
Using D and US size 5 (3.75 mm) needles, cast on 25 sts.
Bind (cast) off.

Bonnet
Using D and US size 5 (3.75 mm) needles, cast on 40 sts for edge of brim and work in garter st (k all rows) as foll:
K4 rows.
Cont in st st, beg with a k row.
Next row: [K2tog] three times, [k1, k2tog] 10 times, k2tog twice. (25 sts)
Work until st st section measures 1 in. (2.5 cm) (approx. 10 rows), ending with RS (k) row.
Back of bonnet:
Next row: *K3, k2tog; rep from * to end. (20 sts)
Cont working in reverse st st as foll:
Next row: P.
Next row: K.
Next row: P.
Next row: *K3, k2tog; rep from * to end. (16 sts)
Work 3 rows in reverse st st as before.
Next row: K2, [k1, k2tog] 4 times, k2. (12 sts)
Break off yarn, thread through rem stitches, and draw up tightly.

Tail

Take a 24-in. (60-cm) length of B and fold in half. With a pencil or similar in the loop and holding the other ends tightly, twist the threads until doubled back on themselves to make a twisted cord; knot this end.

Finishing

Use a yarn sewing needle and mattress stitch for sewing the body, head, arms, cardigan seams.

To make up the Body, with RS tog pull up sts at center of base tightly and, matching patterns and garter stitch rows, sew together. Approx. 1½ in. (4 cm) above skirt border patt, insert tail with knot on WS and incorporate when joining. Cont to join until neck opening.

With WS of Feet together, fold each foot piece in half. With curved edges together, sew around the edge with small neat stitches. Attach folded edge to base of mouse body either side of back seam line, with curved edges facing forward.

Sew hat crown, leaving brim edges open.

Sew Head from snout to back of Head using mattress st and leave opening for stuffing (when stuffing, use tweezers to reach tip of snout).

Fit hat onto head.

Gathered bound- (cast-) off edge of ears and with RS facing forward, attach ears to head by sewing them through hat.

Using black yarn, make eyes using small stitches and carrying thread through head to give suggestion of eye sockets. With pink yarn, embroider tip of snout and mouth.

Attach Head to Body.

Stuff Arms.

Sew Cardigan front from neck to dec. Fit onto Body and attach arms (pin them in place first to find best position) by sewing through Body. Where arms attach you can introduce some shaping to torso. Sew on buttons.

Attach Arms to Body at wrists, using small stitches, to keep Arms flat against Body.

Fold Handbag in half and sew edges neatly as for Feet. Attach handle and attach under Hand.

Attach Scarf at neck as in photo.

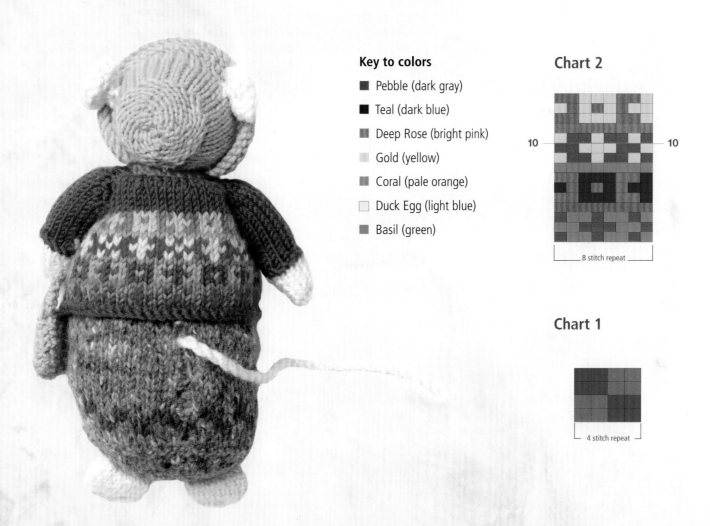

Key to colors

- ■ Pebble (dark gray)
- ■ Teal (dark blue)
- ■ Deep Rose (bright pink)
- □ Gold (yellow)
- ■ Coral (pale orange)
- □ Duck Egg (light blue)
- ■ Basil (green)

Chart 2

10 — ... — 10

8 stitch repeat

Chart 1

4 stitch repeat

cafetière cover

Brighten up your coffee morning with this Fair Isle cafetière cover. It's a good project for a beginner, because it's quite small and the pattern is simple.

materials

- Debbie Bliss Rialto DK (100% extra-fine merino wool) light worsted (DK) yarn
  1 x 1¾ oz (50 g) ball – approx. 115 yd (105 m) – each of shades 58 Grass (green) (A), 02 Ecru (off-white) (B), 50 Deep Rose (pink) (C)
- US size 6 (4 mm) knitting needles
- Yarn sewing needle
- 1 medium off-white button

gauge (tension)

27 sts x 25 rows over 4 in. (10 cm) square working Fair Isle patt in st st using US size 6 (4 mm) needles.

finished size

To fit: standard 3-cup cafetière
Size: 12½ x 6½ in. (31.5 x 16.5 cm)

Notes

Chart is read right to left on odd-numbered (RS) rows and left to right on even-numbered (WS) rows.
Strand colors not in use loosely on WS of work.

Cover

Using A, cast on 77 sts.
Row 1: [K1, p1] to last st, k1 (seed/moss st).
Rep Row 1 three times more. (4 rows)
Follow rows of Chart for first and last edge sts, following repeat across rows and using A, B, C as directed. (77 sts, 32 rows)
Next 4 rows: Work in seed (moss) st.
Bind (cast) off, leave last st on needle.
With RS facing, pick up and k a further 21 sts along row ends of first side of cover, turn.
Work 2 rows seed (moss) st on 22 sts.
Next row: K to end.
Work buttonhole:
Cast on 7 sts and work next 2 rows on these 7 sts only.
Next row: K to end, turn, wyib k2, bind (cast) off 3 sts, k to end.
Next row: K2, turn, wyib cast on 3 sts, turn, k2.
Working on all sts on needle, k to end.
Bind (cast) off.
With RS facing, join in A, pick up and knit 22 sts along row ends of second side of cover.
Work 2 rows seed (moss) st.
K 2 rows.
Bind (cast) off.

Finishing

Block and lightly press.
Sew in ends and sew on button. Catch together opening at top edge with a few stitches.

Key to colors

■ Grass (green)
□ Ecru (off-white)
■ Deep Rose (pink)

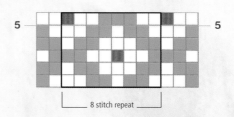

5   5

8 stitch repeat

chunky pillow cover

This is such a beautiful yarn, made from alpaca and merino wool. It's super soft and the strands are like French knitting, which makes a very plump, cozy pillow (cushion).

materials

- Debbie Bliss Paloma (60% baby alpaca/40% merino wool) bulky yarn
    - 4 x 1¾ oz (50 g) hanks – approx. 71 yd (65 m) per ball – of shade 001 White (MC)
    - 1 x 1¾ oz (50 g) hank – approx. 71 yd (65 m) – each of shade 26 Lime (yellow-green), 25 Soft Green (pale blue)
- US size 15 (10 mm) knitting needles
- 18 in. (45 cm) pillow form (cushion pad)
- Yarn sewing needle

gauge (tension)

11 sts x 14 rows over 4 in. (10 cm) square working st st using US size 15 (10 mm) needles.

finished size

To fit 18 in. (45 cm) square pillow form (cushion pad)

Key to colors

▨ Lime (yellow-green)   ▨ Soft Green (pale blue)   ▢ White

Notes

Chart is read right to left on odd-numbered (RS) rows and left to right on even-numbered (WS) rows.

Divide the ball of green into two smaller balls and use one ball for each section of green.

Divide the ball of blue into three smaller balls and use one ball for each section of blue. It's not necessary to divide the white—when not in use strand it loosely on WS of work.

This yarn is very stretchy, so strand yarns loosely across the back and knit plain/unpatterned rows a little more tightly to compensate for Fair Isle rows being a little tighter.

Front and Back

(make 2 the same)

Using MC, cast on 51 sts.

Starting with a p row, work in st st for 17 rows.

Follow Chart to end, using colors as directed.

Using MC, work in st st for 17 rows.

Bind (cast) off.

Finishing

Block and lightly press both pieces.

With WS together, join side and bottom seams with mattress stitch.

Insert pillow form (cushion pad) and sew top seam.

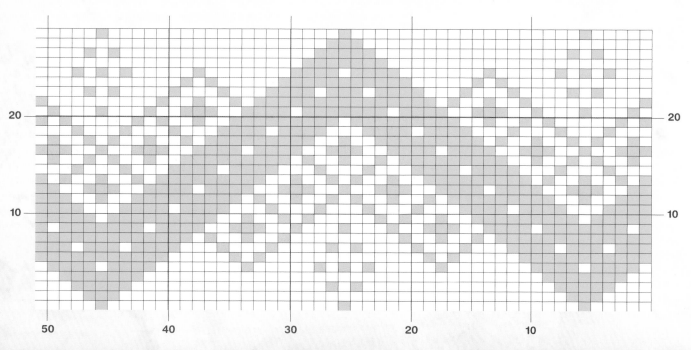

nordic blue pillow cover

A very pretty pillow (cushion) cover using contrast colors. This cover only has Fair Isle on the front and a plain back—but if you would like to brighten up the back make it in stripes instead or repeat the Fair Isle design.

materials

- Debbie Bliss Rialto DK (100% extra-fine merino wool) light worsted (DK) yarn

    4 x 1¾ oz (50 g) balls – approx. 115 yd (105 m) per ball – of shade 20 Teal (dark blue) (MC)

    1 x 1¾ oz (50 g) ball – approx. 115 yd (105 m) – each of shades 48 Maroon (dark pink), 44 Aqua (pale blue), 42 Pink (pale pink), 09 Apple (green), 45 Gold (yellow), 050 Deep Rose (bright pink)

- US size 6 (4 mm) knitting needles
- Yarn sewing needle
- 16 in. (41 cm) pillow form (cushion pad)

gauge (tension)

21 sts and 24 rows over 4 in. (10 cm) square working st st using US size 6 (4 mm) needles.

finished size

To fit a 16 in. (41 cm) pillow form (cushion pad)

Notes
The Chart is read right to left on odd-numbered (RS) rows and left to right on even-numbered (WS) rows.
Strand colors not in use loosely on WS of work.
The cushion cover may come up smaller than 16 in. (41 cm), but once the pillow form (cushion pad) has been fitted inside the stitches stretch out slightly to show off the design.

Front

Using MC and US size 6 (4 mm) needles, cast on 81 sts.
Row 1: K to end.
Row 2: P to end.
Rows 3–92: Foll Chart using st st throughout.
When all 90 rows of Chart have been completed, work 2 rows in st st using MC.
Bind (cast) off.

Back

Using MC and US size 6 (4 mm) needles, cast on 81 sts.
Work in st st until work measures 16 in. (41 cm) or to match Front.
Bind (cast) off.

Finishing
Block and lightly press.
With WS facing, join sides and bottom seams using mattress stitch.
Insert pillow form (cushion pad) and then join top seam using mattress stitch.

top tip

If you make an error and find you have the wrong color of stitch in a small part of the design, instead of unpicking try going back over it later using the Swiss Darning technique (see page 121).

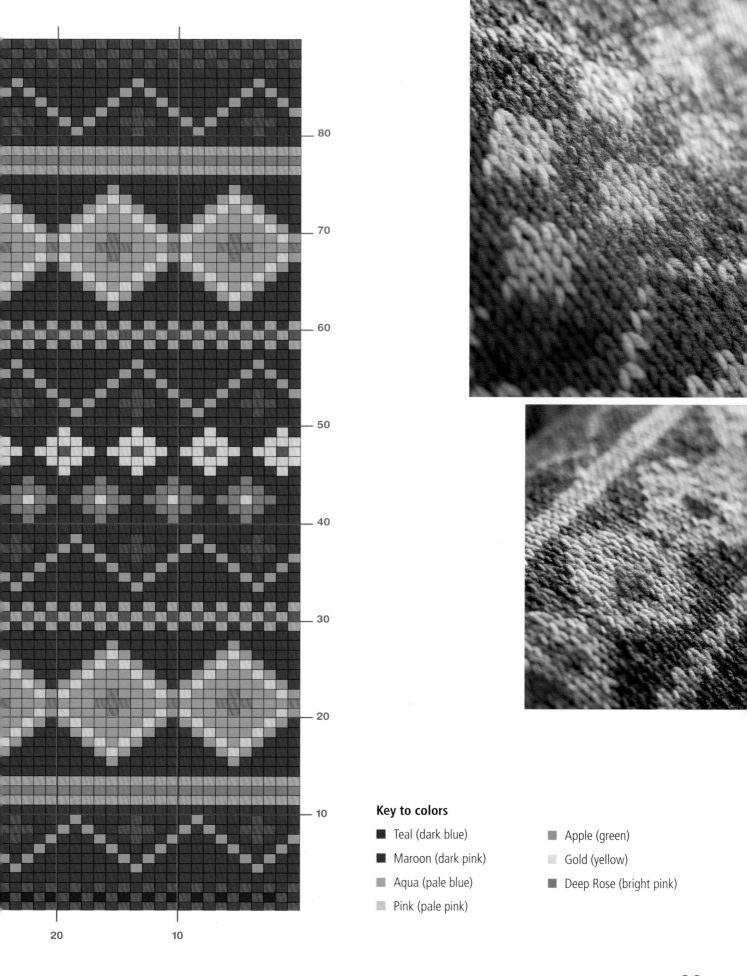

Key to colors

■ Teal (dark blue)

■ Maroon (dark pink)

■ Aqua (pale blue)

□ Pink (pale pink)

■ Apple (green)

□ Gold (yellow)

■ Deep Rose (bright pink)

pastel washcloths

Washcloths are great to knit just for the joy of it. They are a good way to practice Fair Isle—you can use any pure cotton yarn and they make great gifts.

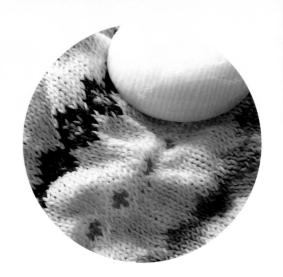

materials

- DMC Natura Just Cotton (100% cotton) thread

Cloth 1:
½ x 1¾ oz (50 g) ball – approx. 85 yd (77.5 m) – of shade N06 Rose Layette (pale pink) (MC)
Small amounts of N76 Bamboo (bright green), N25 Aguamarina (turquoise), N02 Ivory (off-white), N19 Topaze (peach), N27 Star Light (dark blue)

Cloth 2:
½ x 1¾ oz (50 g) ball – approx. 85 yd (77.5 m) – of shade N25 Aguamarina (turquoise) (MC)
Small amounts of N19 Topaze (peach), N02 Ivory (off-white), N42 Paille (pale green/yellow), N23 Passion (orange), N06 Rose Layette (pale pink)

- US size 3 (3.25 mm) knitting needles

gauge (tension)

28.5 sts x 32 rows over 4 in. (10 cm) square working Fair Isle patt in st st using US size 3 (3.25 mm) needles.

finished size

Approx. 8½ in. (21.5 cm) square

Notes
Chart is read right to left on odd-numbered (RS) rows and left to right on even-numbered (WS) rows.
Strand colors not in use loosely on WS of work.

Cloth
Using MC, cast on 57 sts.
Work 4 rows of seed (moss) stitch as follows: [k1, p1] to last st, k1.
Follow Chart to end.
Work 4 rows of seed (moss) st.
Bind (cast) off.

Finishing
Block and press cloths.

top tip
Remember to block the Fair Isle piece, pinning it to size and easing the edges so they are nice and straight (see page 124). This will highlight the pattern to best advantage.

Cloth 1

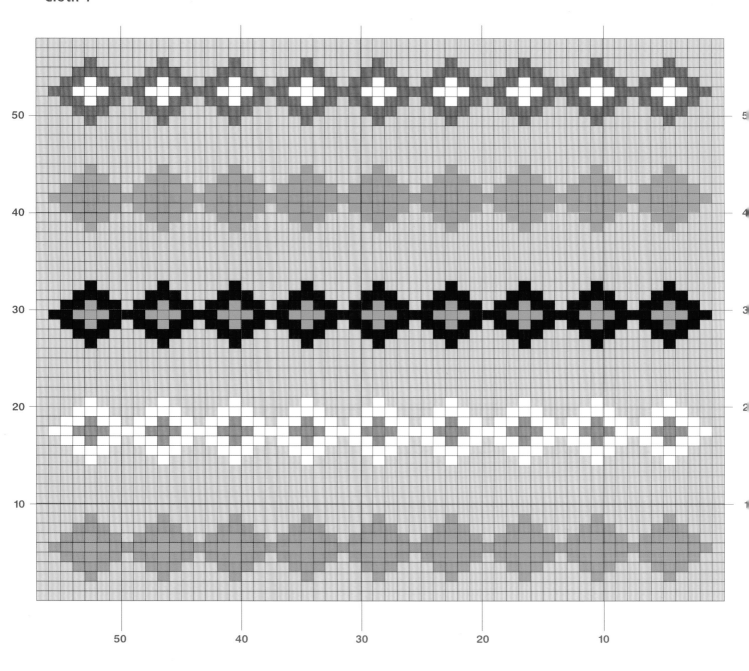

Key to colors

Rose Layette (pale pink) Aguamarina (turquoise) Topaze (peach)

Bamboo (bright green) Ivory (off-white) Star Light (dark blue)

Cloth 2

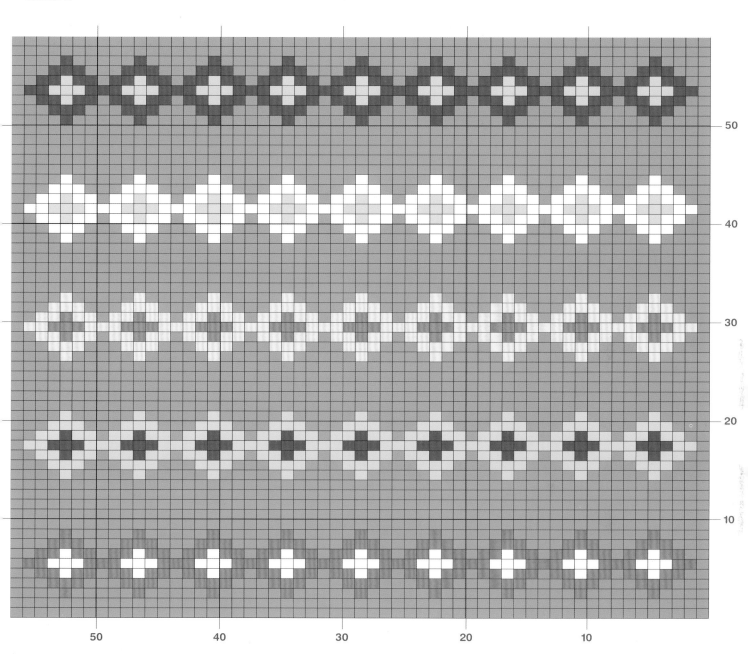

Key to colours

▓ Aguamarina (turquoise)	☐ Ivory (off-white)	▓ Passion (orange)
▓ Topaze (peach)	▓ Paille (pale green/yellow)	▓ Rose Layette (pale pink)

knitted sampler

Fair Isle is not just knitting, it's an art—so why not frame it? This is great way to use up any samples that you may have made for practice, too.

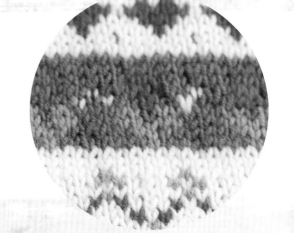

materials

- Debbie Bliss Rialto 4-ply (100% extra-fine merino wool) fingering (4-ply) yarn
  1 x 1¾ oz (50 g) ball – approx. 197 yd (180 m) – each of shades 02 Ecru (off-white) (MC), 18 Teal (blue-green), 22 Fuchsia (bright pink), 32 Leaf (green), 40 Peach Melba (peach), 33 Hyacinth (cornflower blue), 09 Red (bright red)
- US size 3 (3.25 mm) knitting needles

gauge (tension)

30 sts x 32 rows over 4 in. (10cm) square working st st using US size 3 (3.25 mm) needles.

finished size

7¼ x 6¾ in. (18 x 17 cm)

Notes
Chart is read right to left on odd-numbered (RS) rows and left to right on even-numbered (WS) rows.
Strand colors not in use loosely on WS of work.

Picture
Using MC, cast on 55 sts.
Using colors as directed and st st, work 54 rows of Chart.
Bind (cast) off.

Finishing
Weave in ends.

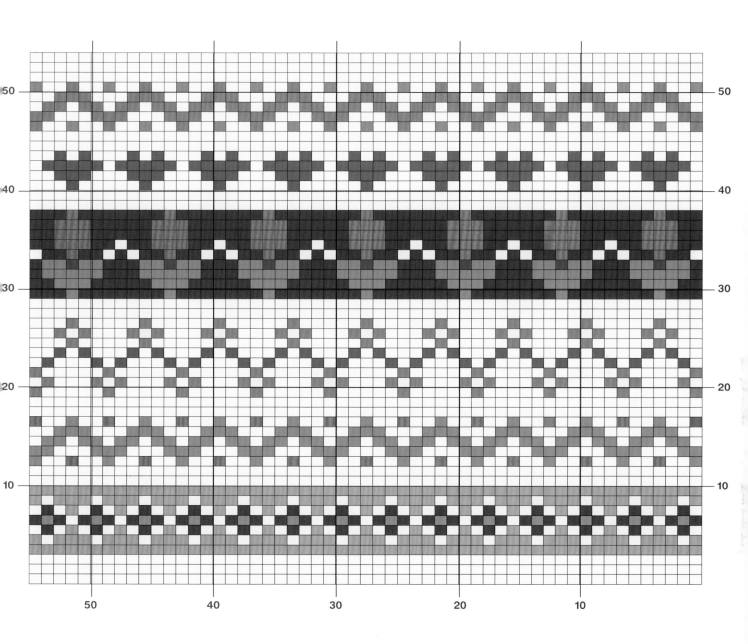

Key to colors

 Ecru (off-white)

■ Teal (blue-green)

■ Fuchsia (bright pink)

■ Leaf (green)

■ Peach Melba (peach)

■ Hyacinth (cornflower blue)

■ Red (bright red)

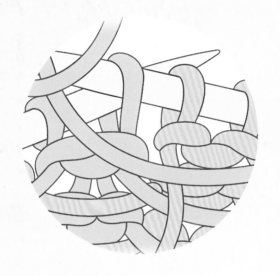

knitting know-how

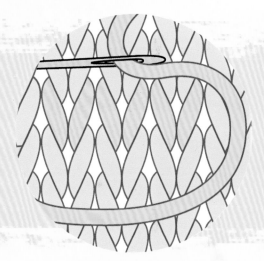

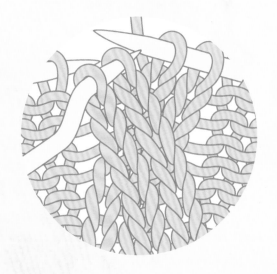

equipment

Knitting needles

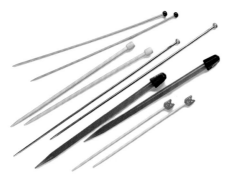

Standard knitting needles can be made of metal, bamboo, wood, or plastic and which type you choose is a matter of personal preference. The different sizes are based on the needle diameter, but they also come in different lengths. Choose shorter needles for smaller projects, because you will find them easier to work with.

Cable needle

These are short needles with a point on each end, used to make a cable pattern in your knitting. Sometimes they have a dip in the middle to help make sure your stitches stay in place on the needle.

Double-pointed and circular needles

Double-pointed needles have a point at both ends and usually come in sets of four, while circular needles consist of a length of flexible cable with a short needle tip at each end. They are both used mainly for knitting in the round to create a tube of fabric, such as when making socks or gloves.

Other equipment

Scissors

A small pair of sharp scissors is a vital tool for all knitters. They are used for snipping the yarn once your work is finished, and for trimming yarn tails after you have woven them in.

Tape measure

A tape measure or ruler is essential for checking your gauge (tension) square and measuring your work.

Yarn sewing needle

Large-eye yarn needles are used to sew your projects together. They are usually slightly blunt so that you do not split the yarn as you sew. Always choose the smallest size possible for the yarn used, because this will make your work easier.

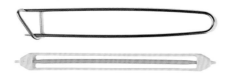

Stitch holders

These are useful to hold a group of stitches while you work on another part of your knitting.

Row counter

Some people find it helpful to have a row counter on one needle so that they can keep track of where they are in their knitting pattern. Alternatively, you could simply make a note with a pencil and a piece of paper.

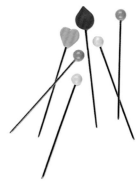

Pins

Pins can be used to hold pieces of knitting together before you sew. You can get special pins for knitting, but any long pins with large heads will work fine.

techniques

Even though there are many Fair Isle techniques to discover, try not to be put off by complicated terms. Here are some techniques that will be useful when making the projects in this book, but remember the projects are there for your guidance and inspiration—use whatever technique suits you best.

Basic knitting

Making a slip knot
You will need to make a slip knot to form your first cast-on stitch.

1 With the ball of yarn on your right, lay the end of the yarn on the palm of your left hand and hold it in place with your left thumb. With your right hand, take the yarn around your top two fingers to form a loop. Take the knitting needle through the back of the loop from right to left and use it to pick up the strand nearest to the yarn ball, as shown in the diagram. Pull the strand through to form a loop at the front.

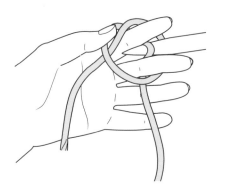

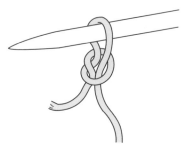

2 Slip the yarn off your fingers, leaving the loop on the needle. Gently pull on both yarn ends to tighten the knot. Then pull on the yarn leading to the ball of yarn to tighten the knot on the needle.

Casting on (cable method)
There are a few methods of casting on, but the one used for most projects in this book is the cable method, which uses two needles.

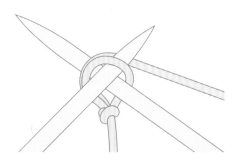

1 Make a slip knot as outlined above. Put the needle with the slip knot into your left hand. Insert the point of your other needle into the front of the slip knot and under the left needle. Wind the yarn from the ball of yarn around the tip of the right needle.

2 Using the tip of your needle, draw the yarn through the slip knot to form a loop. This loop is your new stitch. Slip the loop from the right needle onto the left needle.

3 To make the next stitch, insert the tip of your right needle between the two stitches. Wind the yarn over the right needle, from left to right, then draw the yarn through to form a loop. Transfer this loop to your left needle. Repeat until you have cast on the right number of stitches for your project.

Making a knit stitch

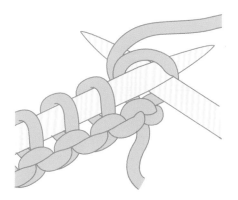  

1 Hold the needle with the cast-on stitches in your left hand, and then insert the tip of the right needle into the front of the first stitch, from left to right. Wind the yarn around the point of the right needle, from left to right.

2 With the tip of your right needle, pull the yarn through the stitch to form a loop. This loop is your new stitch.

3 Slip the original stitch off the left needle by gently pulling your right needle to the right. Repeat these steps until you have knitted all the stitches on your left needle. To work the next row, transfer the needle with all the stitches into your left hand.

Making a knit stitch— continental style

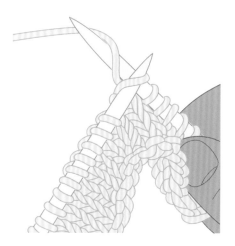 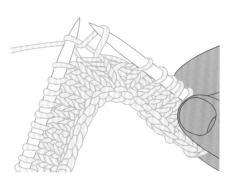 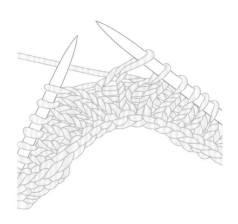

1 Hold the needle with the stitches to be knitted in your left hand, and then insert the tip of the right needle into the front of the first stitch from left to right. Holding the yarn fairly taut with your left hand at the back of your work, use the tip of your right needle to pick up a loop of yarn.

2 With the tip of your right needle, bring the yarn through the original stitch to form a loop. This loop is your new stitch.

3 Slip the original stitch off the left needle by gently pulling your right needle to the right. Repeat these steps until you have knitted all the stitches on your left needle. To work the next row, transfer the needle with all the stitches into your left hand.

Making a purl stitch

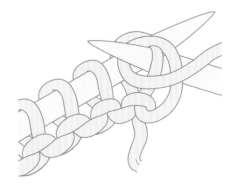

1 Hold the needle with the stitches in your left hand, and then insert the tip of the right needle into the front of the first stitch, from right to left. Wind the yarn around the point of the right needle, from right to left.

2 With the tip of the right needle, pull the yarn through the stitch to form a loop. This loop is your new stitch.

3 Slip the original stitch off the left needle by gently pulling your right needle to the right. Repeat these steps until you have purled all the stitches on your left needle. To work the next row, transfer the needle with all the stitches into your left hand.

Making a purl stitch—continental style

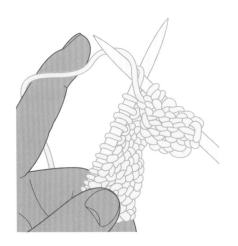

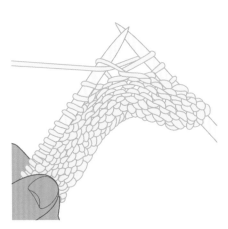

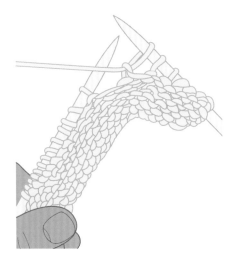

1 Hold the needle with the stitches to be knitted in your left hand, and then insert the tip of the right needle into the front of the first stitch from right to left. Holding the yarn fairly taut at the back of your work, use the tip of your right needle to pick up a loop of yarn.

2 With the tip of your right needle, bring the yarn through the original stitch to form a loop.

3 Slip the original stitch off the left needle by gently pulling your right needle to the right. Repeat these steps until you have purled all the stitches on your left needle. To work the next row, transfer the needle with all the stitches into your left hand.

Binding (casting) off

In most cases, you will bind (cast) off knitwise, which means that you will knit the stitches before you bind (cast) them off.

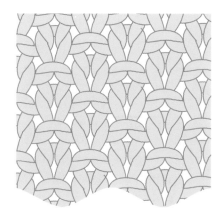

1 First knit two stitches in the normal way. With the point of your left needle, pick up the first stitch you have just knitted and lift it over the second stitch. Knit another stitch so that there are two stitches on your needle again. Repeat the process of lifting the first stitch over the second stitch. Continue this process until there is just one stitch remaining on the right needle.

2 Break the yarn, leaving a tail of yarn long enough to stitch your work together. Pull the tail all the way through the last stitch. Slip the stitch off the needle and pull it fairly tightly to make sure it is secure.

Seed stitch

This is also called moss stitch. On an odd number of stitches, work alternate knit and purl stitches to the last stitch, then knit the last stitch. Repeat this row to make a textured, reversible fabric with alternating smooth and ridged stitches.

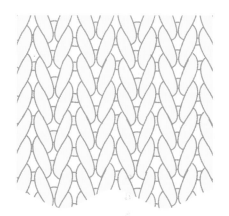

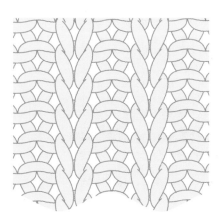

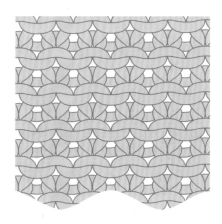

Stockinette (stocking) stitch

This stitch makes a fabric that is different on each side; the knit side is flat and the purl side is textured. To make this stitch, work alternate rows of knit and purl stitches. The front of the fabric is the side on which to work the knit rows.

Ribbing

On an odd number of stitches, alternate knit and purl to the last stitch, and knit the last stitch. On the next row, alternate purl and knit to the last stitch, and purl the last stitch. The smooth and ridged stitches line up to make a reversible elastic fabric.

Garter stitch

This stitch forms a ridged fabric that is the same on both sides. To make this stitch, you simply knit every row.

Working a gauge (tension) swatch

Always try out your Fair Isle gauge (tension)—it can be tighter than on your normal stockinette (stocking) stitch. If you find your Fair Isle rows are tighter than the one-color rows, try to knit the Fair Isle looser and the one-color rows tighter to compensate.

The gauge (tension) is given as the number of stitches and rows you need to work to produce a 4-in. (10-cm) square of knitting.

1 Using the recommended yarn and needles, cast on 8 stitches more than the gauge (tension) instruction asks for—so if you need to have 10 stitches to 4 in. (10 cm), cast on 18 stitches. Working in pattern as instructed, work eight rows more than is needed. Bind (cast) off loosely.

2 Lay the swatch flat without stretching it (the gauge/tension is given before washing or felting). Lay a ruler across the stitches as shown, with the 2-in. (5-cm) mark centered on the knitting, then put a pin in the knitting at the start of the ruler and at the 4-in. (10-cm) mark: the pins should be well away from the edges of the swatch. Count

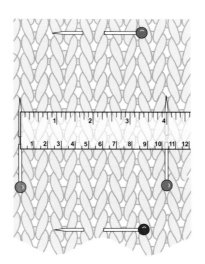

the number of stitches between the pins. Repeat the process across the rows to count the number of rows to 4 in. (10 cm).

If the number of stitches and rows you've counted is the same as the number asked for in the instructions, you have the correct gauge (tension). If you do not have the same number, then you will need to change your gauge (tension).

To change gauge (tension) you need to change the size of your knitting needles. A good rule of thumb to follow is that one difference in needle size will create a difference of one stitch in the gauge (tension). You will need to use larger needles to achieve fewer stitches and smaller ones to achieve more stitches.

Shaping

You can shape your knitting pieces by increasing or decreasing the number of stitches on your needle. Each method results in a slightly different look.

Increasing
Two methods of increasing are used in this book.

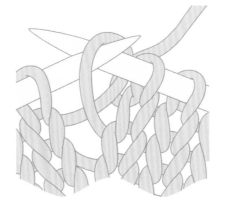

Make 1
Pick up the horizontal strand between two stitches on your left-hand needle. Knit into the back of the loop and transfer the stitch to the right-hand needle in the normal way. (It is important to knit into the back of the loop so that the yarn is twisted and does not form a hole in your work.)

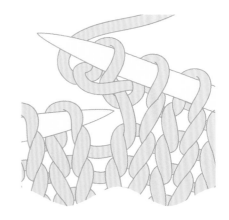

Increase 1
Start knitting your stitch in the normal way but instead of slipping the "old" stitch off the needle, knit into the back of it and then slip the "old" stitch off the needle in the normal way.

Decreasing

There are several ways of decreasing.

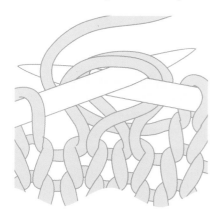

k2tog

This is the simplest way of decreasing. Simply insert your needle through two stitches instead of the normal one when you begin your stitch and then knit them in the normal way.

p2tog

Simply insert your needle through two stitches instead of one when you begin your stitch and then purl them in the normal way.

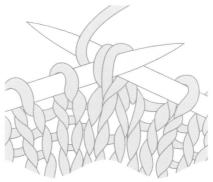
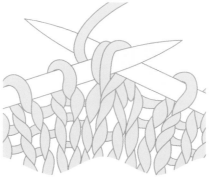

ssk

Slip one stitch and then the next stitch onto your right-hand needle, without knitting them. Then insert the left-hand needle from left to right through the front loops of both the slipped stitches and knit them as normal.

Slipping a stitch

Sometimes you will need to transfer a stitch from the right needle to the left needle, without knitting it. This is known as slipping a stitch and the instruction is written as S1.

To slip a stitch, you simply insert your right-hand needle into the stitch in the normal way as if you were knitting it. Then instead of knitting the stitch, simply pull your right-hand needle further to the right so that the stitch "falls" off the left-hand needle and is transferred to the right-hand needle.

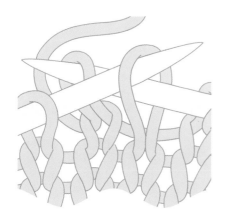

skpo

Slip 1, knit 1, pass slipped stitch over
Slip the first stitch knitwise, knit the next stitch, then use the tip of the left needle to lift the slipped stitch over and off the right needle. The first stitch lies on top, and the decrease slants toward the left.

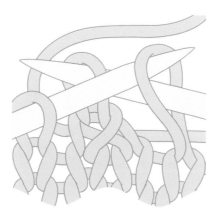

s1, k2tog, psso

This is a way of decreasing two stitches at a time. Slip the first stitch from the left to the right needle without knitting it. Knit the next two stitches together as described above. Then lift the slipped stitch over the stitch in front.

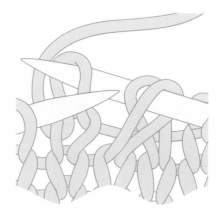

sl 2 k1 psso

Slip 2, knit 1, pass slipped stitches over
Insert right needle through the fronts of the first 2 stitches on left needle as if to knit two together, but slip these stitches onto the right needle; knit the next stitch, then use the tip of the left needle to lift the 2 slipped stitches over and off the right needle. The center stitch lies on top.

Joining

Mattress stitch

There are two versions of this stitch—one used to join two vertical edges and the other used to join two horizontal edges.

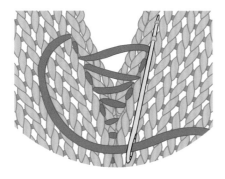
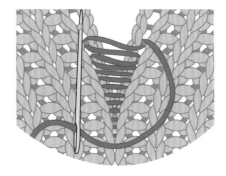

Vertical edges: Place the two edges side by side, with the right side facing you. Take your needle under the running thread between the first two stitches of one side, then under the corresponding running thread of the other side. Pull your yarn up fairly firmly every few stitches.

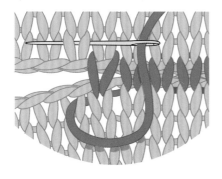
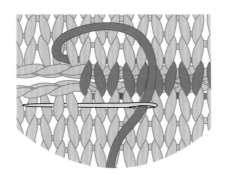

Horizontal edges: Place the two edges side by side, with the right side facing you. Take your needle under the two "legs" of the last row of stitches on the first piece of knitting. Then take your needle under the two "legs" of the corresponding stitch on the second piece of knitting. Pull your yarn up fairly firmly every few stitches.

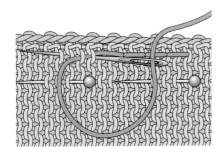
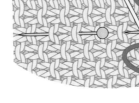

Backstitch seam

This seam is made with right sides facing. Carefully match pattern to pattern, row to row and stitch to stitch. Sew along the seam using backstitch, sewing into the center of each stitch to correspond with the stitch on the opposite piece. Sew as close in from the edge of the knitting as possible to avoid a bulky seam.

Oversewing

This stitch is used to seam small pieces of work. It is normally worked with the right sides of your work together. Take the yarn from the back of your work, over the edge of the seam and out through the back again a short distance further on.

yarn

The specific yarn required for each project is given in the instructions. You can substitute other yarns for those specified, but always make sure that the yarn you use is the same thickness, is made of a similar mix of fibers, and knits up to the recommended gauge (tension).

Substituting yarn

Balls of two different brands of the same type of yarn won't necessarily contain the same quantity of yarn—even if the balls weigh the same, it's the yardage (meterage) that's important. If the substitute yarn has a different yardage (meterage) per ball to the pattern yarn, then you need to do a sum to work out how many balls to buy.

1 Multiply the yardage (meterage) in one ball of pattern yarn by the number of balls needed to find out the total yardage (meterage) of yarn required.

2 Then divide the total yardage (meterage) by the yardage (meterage) in one ball of the substitute yarn to find out how many balls of that yarn you need to buy.

Example:
The pattern yarn has 109 yd (100 m) of yarn in each ball and you need 13 balls.
109 (100) x 13 = 1417 yd (1300 m) of yarn needed in total.

The substitute yarn has 123 yd (112 m) of yarn in each ball.
1417 ÷ 123 = 11.52 (1300 ÷ 112 = 11.6). So you need to buy 12 balls of the substitute yarn.

Before buying all the substitute yarn, buy just one ball and knit a gauge (tension) swatch to be absolutely certain that you can get the right gauge (tension) with that yarn.

fair isle and cable techniques

The following techniques are more specific to the projects in this book, so read through this section before beginning to work.

Stranding

When the color changes are close together you can simply carry the yarn you are not using across the back of the work, picking it up when you need it, leaving a strand or "float" of yarn on the wrong side of the work.

Knit three to five stitches, no more than 1 in. (2.5 cm), of one color (depending on the pattern), then drop the first color and bring in the second. The floats at the back should be carried along loosely. If you spread the stitches out evenly while you make the float this will help avoid puckering, a common problem when knitting Fair Isle. Puckering is caused by the floats being too tight so the work bunches up at the front. It's much easier to sort out longer floats than shorter ones.

Strand from the right side (knit)

1 Knit with the first color for three stitches until the second color is needed (if more stitches are needed in one color, then use the weaving method on page 120). Drop the first color, and then pick up the second color. The new color you are about to knit with will be stranded over the top of the old color.

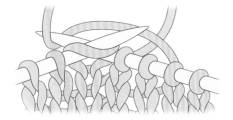

2 Knit the next stitch with the second color. Remember to keep the stranded yarn loose so that the front of the piece does not pucker. Leave the stranded yarn at the back of the work. When you're ready to knit again with the first color, gently pull the first color across and knit with it.

Stranding from the wrong side (purl)

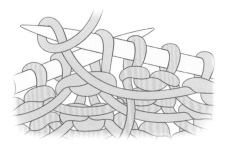

1 Purl with the first color until you need the second color. Drop the first color, pick up the second color, and bring it over the top of the first color. Purl the next stitch with the second color. The stranded yarn should rest easily on the purl side of the work.

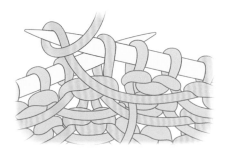

2 When you are ready to purl with the first color again, pull the first color along and purl the next stitch.

Weaving

If the pattern calls for more than three stitches of a single color, then you will need to twist the yarn on the wrong side of the work to prevent long floats and carry the non-used color along ready for knitting when instructed in the pattern.

The yarn that you are not using is twisted around the color that you're working with. Alternate between twisting clockwise and anticlockwise to prevent the yarn from getting too tangled up.

Twisting on the right side

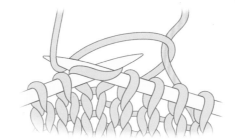

Twisting on the wrong side

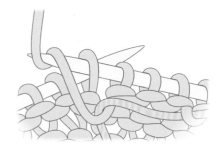

Jogless stripe

A "jog" is created when knitting from one round to the next when the ends of each round don't stay lined up. As you knit up any item in the round using circular needles, you will notice that if you change colors at the beginning of a new round the color and/or pattern tends to fall out of alignment at that point. This is because when you knit in the round you are knitting a spiral, so the beginning and end of a round never perfectly meet.

To avoid this problem on stripe/solid sections, work the jogless stripe technique as follows:

Join in the new color in the first stitch at the beginning of a round and place a stitch marker. Finish knitting in the round to the end as instructed.

Commence the next round by picking up the stitch below the first stitch of the previous round (old color), slip the picked-up stitch onto the left-hand needle and knit together the slipped stitch and the first stitch of the next round.

Long tail cast on

This is a great technique for casting on when knitting socks. It gives a loose gauge (tension) and more stretch. Allow approx 12 in. (30 cm) of tail for every 20 stitches (½—1 in./1–2 cm) of tail per stitch.

1 Leaving a long tail, make a slip knot and place it on a needle. With your palm facing toward you, drape the long tail of yarn over your thumb and the other end (joining the ball) over your index finger. Hold the two strands in place with your other fingers, toward your palm.

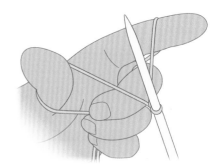

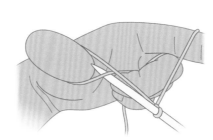

2 Place the needle under the horizontal strand going round the outside of the thumb.

3 Take the needle over and then under the strand coming down from the index finger.

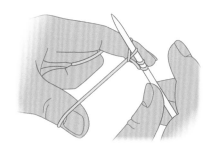

4 Bring the needle through the center of the loop around the thumb.

5 Release the thumb loop and use the long tail to tighten the stitch. Reloop the long tail around the thumb, and repeat from step 1 to make further stitches.

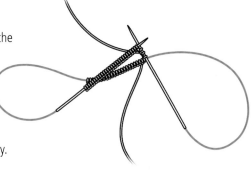

Magic loop

This cast on technique is useful for knitting in the round with circular needles. Cast on the stitches and divide them in half equally, placing half on one needle and the rest on the cord. Pull a length of the cord through the gap between the two sets of stitches, ensuring that the row is not twisted. Join for working in the round by placing a marker for the first stitch of the round, then pull the right-hand needle slightly out of its stitches, while leaving the other half of the stitches on the left-hand needle. Knit the stitches from the left-hand needle as usual using the right-hand needle, and pulling tightly on the yarn for the first couple of stitches to ensure that the round joins seamlessly. The right-hand needle will now have stitches on it and the left-hand needle will not. Pull the cord so that the stitches on it are on the left-hand needle and then pull out the right-hand needle, leaving its stitches on the cord, so that you can use it to knit off the left-hand needle.

Swiss darning

Sometimes it's easier to place one stitch using the Swiss darning technique rather than weaving or stranding a second or third color across a row/round. Swiss darning (also known as duplicate stitch) is a brilliant technique in which you embroider a new color over the top of one or more stitch(es). It's also a really useful technique if you've knitted one (or two) of your stitches in the wrong color.

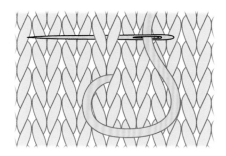

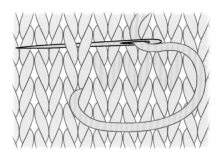

1 Insert a darning/tapestry needle from the wrong side of the work and bring the yarn up in the center of the stitch to be worked on. Take the needle from the right to the left behind both sides of the stitch above the one being worked on, and pull the yarn through.

2 Complete by taking the needle back through where you began.

3 Work from right to left as shown.

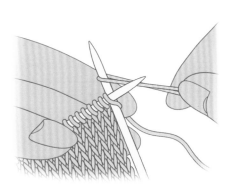
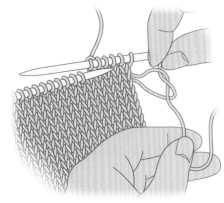

Joining in a new color

You will usually bring in a new color (as directed in the pattern or chart) at the beginning of the row/round. Break the old yarn, leaving a 4–6 in. (10–15 cm) tail. Insert the needle into the next stitch to be knitted, then knit in the new color as usual, leaving a 4–6 in. (10–15 cm) tail. These tails can be tied together to hold them in position and to stop the loose stitch from falling off the needle. I usually knit one or two stitches before I tie them in place. Never tie in a double knot, because this will make it difficult to sew in the end later and the knot will eventually work itself out of your work.

Sewing in ends

When working Fair Isle you will usually be working with lots of different colors, so you will need to sew in your ends neatly at the back. Use a yarn sewing needle with a large enough eye to thread the tail of your yarn. Weave the tails along the wrong side of the work loosely for approx. 2 in. (5 cm), working in and out of the same color as your tail if possible.

Understanding charts

When reading patterns and charts for Fair Isle knitting, it's important to read through the whole pattern first. Some patterns will have the whole chart for you to follow and others will have smaller chart "repeats"—sections that will need to be knitted across the row/round. Repeats are indicated on the chart by a thick black line. The part of the chart on each side of the repeat is to be followed for the beginning and end of the row/round.

In this book we have color-coordinated each chart to match the yarn colors I've chosen on each of the projects, which make the charts really easy to read. The Fair Isle patterns are knitted using stockinette (stocking) stitch. The charts do not specify which row/round is knit (RS) and which is purl (WS), so make sure you alternate knit/purl rows as you work each chart. Instructions will be in the text of each individual project.

If you're knitting in the round (on circular needles), read the chart from right to left and from bottom to top. If you're knitting in rows, read every odd-numbered row from right to left, knitting each stitch (right side), and then every even-numbered row from left to right, purling each stitch (wrong side).

Knit tightly in the one-color stockinette (stocking) stitch rows to balance out the gauge (tension) difference with the stranded colorwork sections, which should be knitted loosely. Follow the text in pattern for increases and decreases.

Tips for keeping your place on the chart

■ Don't be afraid to make marks all over your charts.

■ If possible, photocopy/scan your chart and mark off each row/round on the chart with a pen or pencil.

■ I use a long glass-headed pin to mark the place on my charts. It means you have puncture marks all over the paper, but it saves the endless pens and pencils that get lost down the side of the sofa.

Intarsia knitting

This is a technique used for knitting colored motifs and shapes. The color is not carried along the row—use separate lengths of yarn for each area of color and twist the two yarns together on the wrong side of the work when they meet. This will make sure that the colors are taken up as you knit and no holes are created. Using this method uses less yarn and creates only a single-layer fabric.

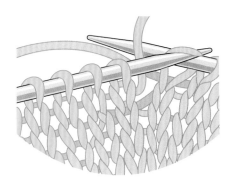

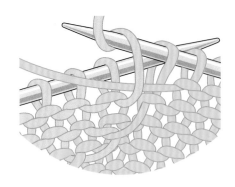

Knit row

Knit the last stitch in the old color, drop the yarn at the back, and pick up the new color, making sure that it loops around the old color. Knit the first stitch in the new color securely so that the joins are neat.

Purl row

Purl the last stitch in the old color. Drop the old color and pick up the new color, looping it around the old color. Purl the next stitch in the new color securely so that the joins are neat.

Using a yarn bobbin

When there are several color changes along a row, it's useful to use a yarn bobbin to avoid the colors getting tangled up. These can be store bought and are made of plastic or card. Wind small amounts of each color you need onto separate bobbins.

Changing colors

You can loop the yarns around one another if the colors change in a straight line up the work. If you are working stripes, change color at the end of row by dropping the old color at the end of the row and knitting the new color at the beginning of the row. You can either cut the old color, leaving a 6-in. (15-cm) tail for sewing in later, or—if the color changes fall on an even number—you can weave

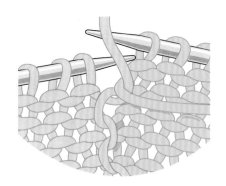

the yarns up the side of the work by winding them around each other, looping them up the side as you knit.

Cables

Create texture and pattern with cables by swapping the order in which you knit stitches. To create the cable, you put a number of stitches on a cable needle and hold them in front (front cable) or behind (back cable) the work and then go back to them. Using a bent cable needle (see page 108) will make it even easier to hold the

group of stitches being moved. The number given in the instruction refers to the total number of stitches over which the cable is being worked—so for C4F (as shown on page 124) you only put two stitches on the cable needle.

Working a four-stitch front cable (C4F)

This is worked over four stitches and will make a cable that twists to the left.

Cable six forward (C6F) is worked in exactly the same way, but hold three stitches at the front on the cable needle in step 1 and work three stitches in step 2.

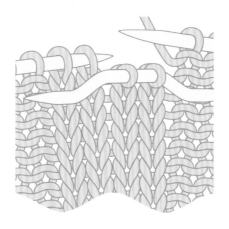

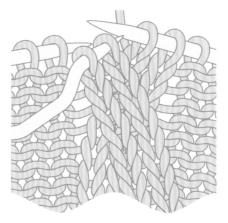

1 Work to the position of the cable. Slip the next two stitches on the left-hand needle onto the cable needle, keeping the cable needle in front of the work. Leave the two stitches on the cable needle in the middle so they don't slip off.

2 Knit the next two stitches off the left-hand needle in the usual way, then knit the two stitches off the cable needle and continue working from your pattern.

Working a six-stitch back cable (C6B)

This is worked over six stitches, but this time the cable needle is held at the back so the cable will twist to the right. First work to the position of the cable as before.

Cable four back (C4B) is worked in exactly the same way, but hold two stitches at the back on the cable needle in step 1 and work two stitches in step 2.

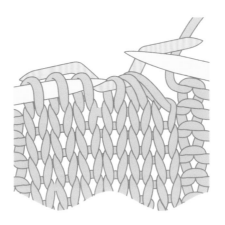

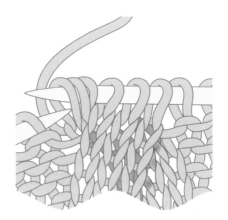

1 Slip the next three stitches on the left-hand needle onto the cable needle, keeping the cable needle at the back of the work. Leave the three stitches on the cable needle in the middle so they don't slip off.

2 Knit the next three stitches of the left-hand needle in the usual way, then knit the three stitches off the cable needle and continue working from your pattern.

Blocking and pressing

Even if your overall knitting gauge (tension) is consistent and the float tension is perfect, Fair Isle knitting can look uneven but blocking will resolve this. Blocking makes a huge difference—you could be pulling your hair out thinking your fabric looks terrible and then a simple block makes it look like the piece of art that it is. Pin your knitted fabric to the correct size, easing it gently as you go, then either press the work using a damp cloth or dampen the work using the steamer on your iron. A few areas may still not be perfectly flat—but remember, this is your own individual work and it will still look beautiful.

Problem-solving tips

Needles—If you are knitting with metal needles, try changing to wooden ones that grip the stitches easier and help keep them spaced out.

Weave in the ends—With so many different loose ends, some can work free. Weave in the ends before you throw your knitted piece away in frustration—it's a great opportunity to tidy things up, repair holes, and straighten edges.

Puckering—Keep checking your work as you work along the row/round. Spread out the stitches on the needle every inch (cm) or so to check that the gauge (tension) is not pulling too much in any of the colors.

abbreviations

alt	alternate
approx	approximately
beg	begin(ning)
CC	contrast color
CN	cable needle
cont	continue
dec	decrease/decreasing
dpns	double pointed needles
foll	follow/following
inc	increase/increasing (see page 114)
k	knit
k2tog	knit 2 stitches together (see page 115)
k2tog tbl	knit 2 stitches together through back of loop
LH	left hand
M1	make a stitch (see page 114)
MC	main color
p	purl
p2tog	purl 2 stitches together (see page 115)
p2tog tbl	purl 2 stitches together through back of loop
patt	pattern
psso	pass slipped stitch over
rem	remain(ing)
rep	repeat
RH	right hand
rib 2tog	rib 2 stitches together
RS	right side
skpo	slip 1 stitch, knit 1 stitch, pass slipped stitch over (see page 115)
sl2 k1 psso	slip 2 stitches, knit 1 stitch, pass slipped stitches over (see page 115)
sl	slip the number of stitches given
ssk	slip 1 stitch, slip 1 stitch, knit the slipped stitches together (see page 115)
st st	stockinette (stocking) stitch
st(s)	stitch(es)
tog	together
WS	wrong side
WS	WS
wyib	with yarn in back
yf	yarn forward
yrn	yarn round needle

suppliers

UK STOCKISTS

Laughing Hens
(wool, accessories)
The Croft Stables
Station Lane
Great Barrow
Cheshire CH3 7JN
01829 740903
www.laughinghens.com

Yarn Companies

Rooster Yarns
The Croft Stables
Station Lane
Great Barrow
Cheshire CH3 7JN
01829 740903
www.roosteryarns.com

Designer Yarns
(Debbie Bliss yarns)
Units 8-10 Newbridge Industrial
Estate
Pitt Street
Keighley
West Yorks BD21 4PQ
01535 664222
www.designeryarns.uk.com

Tuition

Nicki Trench Workshops
Crochet, knitting, and craft
workshops for all levels.
Email: nicki@nickitrench.com
Blog: nickitrench.blogspot.co.uk

US STOCKISTS

Knitting Fever
(Debbie Bliss yarns)
www.knittingfever.com

The Knitting Garden
(Debbie Bliss yarns)
www.theknittinggarden.com

One Planet Yarn & Fiber
(Artesano yarns)
www.oneplanetyarnandfiber.com

Webs
(yarn, accessories)
www.yarn.com

Yarn Market
(yarn, accessories)
www.yarnmarket.com

Accessories

A.C. Moore
Stores nationwide
1-888-226-6673
www.acmoore.com

Hobby Lobby
Online store and stores
nationwide
www.shop.hobbylobby.com
www.hobbylobby.com

Jo-Ann Fabric and Craft Store
1-888-739-4120
www.joann.com

Michaels
Stores nationwide
1-800-642-4235
www.michaels.com

index

acknowledgments

Writing and designing a Fair Isle book has presented lots of challenges. I've been able to use some amazingly talented knitters and have had endless support and help from all of my team to whom I'm forever grateful. They are:

The knitters: Tracey Elks, Bronagh Miskelly, Janice Issitt, Mel Howes, Tina McAra, Frances Jago, Helen Metcalf, Helen Burridge, Jo Bodley, Holly Gunning, and Carolyn Meggison.

My special thanks go to Bronagh Miskelly who graded patterns, wrote charts, and worked endlessly trying to get shapes and my designs into order. And I'd like to thank Marilyn Wilson for her meticulous pattern checking.

Also big thanks to Ian Watt, Rhiannon Evans, Dionne Taylor, and Nicole Bennett from Designer Yarns, who supplied the majority of the beautiful yarn for the projects in this book. For other yarns, thanks to Rooster Yarns and Artesano Yarns.

Thanks as always to Marie Clayton for her brilliant editing and to Penny Craig at CICO Books for her commitment to the charts! And thanks to Cindy Richards at CICO for commissioning such a lovely book, it's been a delight to work on.

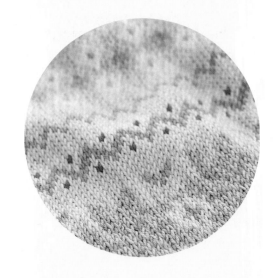